Crisis Intervention

Neil Thompson

 Theory into Practice
Series Editor Neil Thompson

Russell House Publishing

First published in 2011 by:
Russell House Publishing Ltd.
4 St George's House
Uplyme Road
Lyme Regis
Dorset
DT7 3LS
Tel: 01297 443948
Fax: 01297 442722
e-mail: help@russellhouse.co.uk
www.russellhouse.co.uk

British Library Cataloguing-in-publication Data:

A catalogue record for this book is available from the British Library.

ISBN: 978-1-905541-67-6

Typeset by: Avenue Media Solutions, Wrexham
Printed by: IQ Laserpress, Aldershot

About Russell House Publishing

Russell House Publishing aims to publish innovative and valuable materials to help managers, practitioners, trainers, educators and students.

Our full catalogue covers: social policy, working with young people, helping children and families, care of older people, social care, combating social exclusion, revitalising communities and working with offenders.

Full details can be found at www.russellhouse.co.uk and we are pleased to send out information to you by post. Our contact details are on this page.

We are always keen to receive feedback on publications and new ideas for future projects

Contents

The Theory into Practice Series

This exciting series fills a significant gap in the market for short, user-friendly texts, written by experts that succinctly introduce sets of theoretical ideas, relate them clearly to practice issues, and guide the reader to further learning. They particularly address discrimination, oppression, equality and diversity. They can be read as general overviews of particular areas of theory and practice or as foundations for further study. The series will be invaluable across the human services, including social work and social care; youth and community work; criminal and community justice work; counselling; advice work; housing; and aspects of health care.

About the Series Editor

Neil Thompson is an internationally known writer, teacher and adviser. He is currently Director of Avenue Consulting Ltd (www.avenueconsulting.co.uk), a company offering training and consultancy to the 'people professions'. He has held full or honorary professorships at four UK universities. He has over 150 publications to his name, including several bestselling textbooks, papers in learned journals and training and open learning materials. He has also produced a number of education and training DVDs (www.avenuemediasolutions.com).

Neil is a Fellow of the Chartered Institute of Personnel and Development; the Royal Society of Arts (elected on the basis of his contribution to organisational learning); and the Higher Education Academy. He was the founding editor of the *British Journal of Occupational Learning* and now edits the US-based international journal, Illness, Crisis & Loss. He is also the editor-in-chief of two online resources:
Well-being Zone (www.well-beingzone.com) and
Social Work Focus (www.socialworkfocus.com).
His personal website is at www.neilthompson.info.

Prospective authors wishing to make a contribution to the *Theory into Practice* series should contact Neil via his company website,
www.avenueconsulting.co.uk.

Series Editor's Foreword

About the series

The relationship between theory and practice is one that has puzzled practitioners and theorists alike for some considerable time, and there still remains considerable doubt about how the two interconnect. However, what is clear is that it is dangerous to tackle the complex problems encountered in 'people work' without having at least a basic understanding of what makes people tick, of how the social context plays a part in both the problems we address and the solutions we seek. Working with people and their problems is demanding work. To try to undertake it without being armed with a sound professional knowledge base is a very risky strategy indeed, and potentially a disastrous one.

An approach to practice based mainly on guesswork, untested assumptions, habit and copying others is clearly not one that can be supported. Good practice must be an *informed* practice, with actions based, as far as possible, on reasoning, understanding and evidence. This series is intended to develop just such good practice by providing:

- an introductory overview of a particular area of theory or professional knowledge;
- an exploration of how it relates to practice issues;
- a consideration of how the theory base can help tackle discrimination and oppression; and
- a guide to further learning.

The texts in the series are written by people with extensive knowledge and practical experience in the fields concerned and are intended as an introduction to the wider and more in-depth literature base.

About this book

Crisis intervention is a long-standing and highly respected approach to helping people in difficulties and distress. Historically, it has its roots in mental health, but it can be used in a wide variety of situations and settings and by a wide range of professionals: social workers and other social care workers; probation officers and youth justice workers; youth and community workers; nurses and other healthcare professionals; counsellors and psychotherapists; police and community support officers; advice workers, mediators and pastoral staff. It can also be of use to managers and leaders at times.

The book is a revised and updated version of *Crisis Intervention Revisited*, first published by Pepar Publications in 1991. It now follows the usual *Theory into Practice* series format and therefore has four parts. The first part explains the theory base behind crisis intervention. This sets the scene for Part Two where the implications for practice are drawn out. In Part Three the emphasis is on tackling discrimination and oppression, while Part Four is a guide to further learning.

The book is intended to show the value of crisis intervention as a helping approach and to provide a foundation for learning more about it so that its benefits for practice can be capitalised upon. It shows that crisis intervention is a helpful, albeit demanding, method of working with people in difficulties and distress – an attempt to capitalise on the positive potential of crisis. This makes it an excellent basis for promoting empowerment.

Neil Thompson, Series Editor

About the author

Neil Thompson is an independent consultant, trainer and author with Avenue Consulting Ltd. His interests include equality and diversity; workplace well-being; loss and grief; and workplace learning. He is a well-published author and his recent books include *People Skills* (3rd edn, Palgrave Macmillan, 2009) and *Loss, Grief and Trauma in the Workplace* (Baywood, 2009d). Neil has a long-standing commitment to the value of crisis intervention as a way of helping people through difficult times.

Acknowledgements

I am grateful to Willie More of Pepar Publications for his support in developing the first edition of this book some years ago. His generosity of spirit was an inspiration. I am also grateful to Geoffrey Mann for his support in developing not only this new edition of the book, but also the *Theory into Practice* series. His comments on the first draft were also very helpful. As always, it has been a pleasure working with him. Thanks are also due to Susan Thompson for her ongoing support in so many ways. I am also grateful to Emeritus Professor Bernard Moss of Staffordshire University for his helpful comments on an earlier draft of the book.

Introduction

It has long been recognised that crises are a very important aspect of working with people in difficulties and distress in general, but just how important, indeed crucial, they can be has not always been fully appreciated.

Crisis intervention is an approach which is premised on the argument that crises are fundamental and highly significant aspects of the situations helping professionals encounter across a variety of settings. Ignoring the nature, basis and implications of crisis can be seen as dangerous, costly and detrimental to good professional practice. It is therefore essential to develop a clear and thorough understanding of crisis-related issues and learn the skills and techniques required to relate such concepts to our practice with people in crisis. The facilitation of just such a process is precisely the aim of this book – a clear and concise introduction to the theory and methods of crisis intervention and the advantages and difficulties associated with adopting such an approach.

The emphasis is strongly on crisis intervention as an applied method. This is neither purely a theoretical treatise nor simply an atheoretical 'commonsense' guide to practice. It is intended as a bridge between theory and practice – a study which takes account of both of these important dimensions and the interaction between the two (see Thompson, 2000a, for a discussion of the complex relationship between theory and practice in general and Thompson, 2010, for discussion of those issues specifically as they relate to social work).

I shall be using the term 'crisis' in a slightly technical sense but the meaning ascribed to it is not very far removed from the everyday 'commonsense' usage of the word. This should become clearer in the pages that follow.

A crisis is a turning point, a situation which pushes our usual coping mechanisms beyond their limits of effectiveness and thus necessitates a different response, a different strategy for coping. Everstine and Everstine (2006) capture this point well when they argue that:

> A person in crisis encounters a situation or series of situations that cause the person to alter his or her patterns of living. The circumstances that lead to each person's crisis moment are unique to the person, but the experience of being-in-crisis is universal – from the cabinet minister to the cabinet maker. The key element in everyone's crisis is disruption in the normal conduct of one's affairs, of change being required of the person by forces beyond control, by the feeling that 'things might never be the same'. (pp. 3-4).

The term 'crisis' is often used in everyday speech to denote a highly stressful set of circumstances or an emergency. However, this rather loose usage of the term is unhelpful, for we need to be precise about what we mean by 'crisis'. The amount of stress, quantitatively speaking, is not necessarily an indicator of crisis. For example, a student may feel considerable pressure or even stress when facing exams, but may none the less cope quite effectively without having to take drastic steps. In other words they may take it in their stride and thus, despite the high level of pressure, a crisis does not arise. For others, however, who may not be so well equipped to handle such pressure, a crisis may be provoked by an even lower level of demand upon them. 'Crisis' is therefore a qualitative concept, rather than simply a quantitative one.

The issues relating to coping abilities, how and why they break down and the consequences of such breakdown will be consistent themes throughout this text. They are key aspects of crisis intervention, for it is in relation to these factors that intervention by a skilled helper can be so fruitful, as indeed we shall see below. Crisis is the 'critical' moment, the time when significant changes can be made as a result of the energy and motivation the situation produces. These changes can prove to be constructive or destructive, helpful or detrimental, and so crisis point is very much a turning point, simultaneously a threat and an opportunity for growth. It is a challenge. It has challenged and defeated the coping mechanisms within our usual repertoire and is now challenging our ability to develop new and effective methods of handling the situation. One of the key roles for the professional helper in crisis intervention is therefore an educative one, to teach people in crisis new and effective responses, to guide them towards the positive and constructive use of crisis.

Very often the response of those close to a person in crisis is to look for a shortcut through the crisis or simply to sit it out. This is often mistakenly referred to as crisis intervention, but this type of 'patching up' of a crisis would be more accurately termed 'crisis survival', as the aim is to minimise damage, rather than maximise the potential for growth and development and progress in dealing with the problems and challenges being faced.

Crisis intervention does not therefore simply mean intervening in crises in a general sense; it is a specific approach to crisis based on a set of theoretical principles, a conceptual framework to guide and inform practice. Crisis intervention is not just one among many 'tools of intervention'. Rather, it provides a framework of understanding that can be used to enhance the use of other methods. This book should not therefore be seen as a study of crisis as a general phenomenon, but rather an introduction to the specific concepts and techniques that are of value to those workers in the helping professions who are called upon to deal with crises.

Chapter 1 presents a brief and schematic account of traditional crisis theory and its key tenets. It also attempts, albeit in outline only, to indicate some weak points of the traditional thinking on the subject and to point to a more sophisticated and updated theoretical basis. This sets the scene for Part Three of the book.

Chapter 2 is concerned with the positive use of crisis, the potential for learning and growth inherent in the challenge of crisis. The chapter begins with an analysis of the physiological concomitants of crisis and from this moves on to examine the usefulness of assertiveness. The chapter also discusses the relationship between crisis theory and other approaches to helping (theories, tools, methods). It provides illustrations of how crisis intervention can be used alongside other theory-based methods. The point emphasised is that crisis intervention is not an exclusive approach; it can be used in tandem with a wide range of other helping methods.

To open Part Two Chapter 3 emphasises the need for timely, clear and accurate assessment and explores some of the skills required and how they can be developed.

Chapter 4 tackles the issues of integrating theory and practice – the 'nuts and bolts' of using crisis theory in practice, as it were. This chapter attempts to paint a picture of what a crisis intervention approach in action actually looks like.

Chapter 5 provides illustrations of the themes and issues so far raised. Three case studies based on actual examples of crisis intervention practice are presented. Links are drawn between the practice situations and the theoretical issues which underpin them.

Chapter 6 explores some of the significant demands that crisis work makes of professional helpers. This chapter is intended to provide a helpful backdrop to the realities of practice. It raises questions about the support networks needed and the organisational implications for workers who seek to adopt a crisis intervention approach.

Chapter 7 is the first of two chapters in Part Three concerned with promoting equality and valuing diversity. Its focus is on crisis intervention in the context of anti-discriminatory practice. Chapter 8 completes Part Three and is concerned with how crisis intervention can be seen as part of a commitment to empowerment.

Following the Guide to Further Learning that forms Part Four is the conclusion. This restates the main themes and draws the discussion to a close, making the point that the art of the crisis worker involves helping to guide people from the pain, grief and hurt of a crisis situation, through compassion and onwards to growth, opportunity and empowerment.

The message I seek to convey in this book is that crisis intervention is a very useful and effective theory-based approach to helping people to deal positively with a wide range of potentially destructive crisis situations. In some respects it is a very demanding approach, but the case I wish to argue here, on the basis of many years' experience of using these methods, is that the benefits of this approach far outweigh the costs in terms of time, energy and emotional commitment. It is to be hoped that the following chapters will succeed in clarifying and justifying this faith in crisis intervention.

Part One: Crisis Theory

Introduction

In keeping with the standard structure of books in the *Theory into Practice* series, Part One provides an overview of the theoretical underpinnings of crisis intervention. It contains two chapters, the first focusing on traditional crisis theory and how it needs to change to be consistent with more recent understandings of people and their problems and with professional values that emphasise the need to value diversity and promote equality and social justice. The second focuses on the positive potential of crisis, emphasising that the role of the crisis worker is to help capitalise on the opportunities for growth, learning and transformation that the crisis situation presents.

It is important to note that what is presented in Part One is merely an introduction to the theory base and should certainly not be seen as in any way comprehensive or exhaustive. It is a beginning, an introduction to a very complex set of issues rather than a full account of them. If your work leads you into situations where you will be helping people who are in crisis, then you are strongly advised to use this book as a stepping stone to a fuller understanding of the issues rather than see it as an adequate basis of understanding in its own right. Part Four provides guidance on how to find out more about this fascinating topic. It lists details of books, journals and relevant organisations and internet resources.

Chapter 1
Crisis Theory: Old and New

Introduction

The theoretical underpinnings of crisis intervention are based on a problem-solving model of human action and learning. Each day we are faced with a range of problems to solve, mostly of a minor nature. In order to cope with this procession of problems we develop a range of coping responses which are variously known as 'mechanisms', 'skills', 'methods', or 'strategies'. This repertoire includes interpersonal skills, stress management techniques and other forms of practical and emotional resourcefulness.

There are two basic dimensions to this process of dealing with problems: the subjective and the objective. The objective element consists of the external factors which go to make up the problem situation – the personal, social and economic circumstances of those involved. The subjective element relates to the 'inner state' of the person(s) concerned – the perceptions, emotions and cognitive processes which contribute to, and respond to, the objective circumstances. Crisis theory makes it clear that the subjective is not simply a reflection of the objective, as if some mechanistic or deterministic process were operating. The technical term for this is 'agency'. Although each of us is heavily influenced by external factors, we none the less have choices to make in terms of how we subjectively make sense of those factors and how we respond to them. That is, we are human 'agents' who interact with the objective circumstances we encounter – we are, of course influenced by those factors but our actions are not entirely determined by them.

The relationship between the subjective and the objective is based on a range of complex psychological and social interactions. The details of this need not concern us here, but the key point from a crisis theory point of view is that dealing with problems has both a subjective and an objective dimension (a subjective 'outlook' based on how the individual perceives the situation and the objective, external circumstances themselves), and consequently the breakdown of coping mechanisms and subsequent development of new coping methods can relate to either or both dimensions. It is a mistake, in terms of both theory and practice, to concentrate on one at the expense of the other.

As was argued earlier, in the Introduction, a crisis is qualitatively different from 'problems' in the general or wider sense. A crisis necessarily involves change or movement as, by definition, conventional 'tactics' have failed or proven inappropriate. Such change can be positive or negative, deterioration or improvement, damage or progress (this theme will be explored more fully in Chapter 2 below). Consequently crisis is characterised by risk and hence tension and anxiety. Such risk and the challenges it entails are therefore important issues, and a practitioner who fails to recognise this may do more harm than good, as his or her intervention also becomes part of the crisis scenario. Practitioners using crisis intervention need to be sensitive to the risks involved and be ready to intervene, where necessary, in maximising the positive potential of the situation.

The following are examples of just some of the wide range of potential crisis situations that members of the helping professions may encounter:

- Family tensions and conflicts reach a point where one or more family members feel they cannot cope any longer and therefore feel the need either to leave the situation or change it quite significantly.
- Someone is diagnosed with a terminal illness or long-term debilitating condition that will drastically change their life.
- A couple decide to separate or divorce, and so their lives cannot carry on as before; both will have to make significant changes.
- Someone experiences a major bereavement, the loss of someone very close to them.
- A family are evicted from their home.
- Someone is hospitalised as a result of a worsening of their mental health problems.
- A child and their parents face major changes when the child is received into care as a result of suspected abuse.
- An elderly person gives up their home when being admitted to a care home.
- Someone is made redundant and does not know how they are going to cope without this major aspect of their life.
- A child is being bullied at school and no longer feels able to face going into school.
- A teenager is arrested for possession of drugs and so their parents throw them out.

In order to help people capitalise on the positive potential of these situations we need to develop an understanding of the characteristics of crisis, and it is to this that we now turn.

Crisis and loss

One of the central concepts relating to crisis is that of loss. This is because (i) crises often arise as a result of a major loss; and (ii) crises can give rise to significant losses. Lindemann's classic study of grief reactions outlined the main responses to a serious loss. From a detailed study of 101 bereaved relatives he detected a pattern consisting largely of the following elements (see Lindemann, 1944,1965):

1. *Somatic distress* Physical symptoms, for example, nausea, debility.
2. *Preoccupation with the deceased's image* A tendency to focus on images or matters relating to the person lost.
3. *Guilt* Self-blame, however irrational, in relation to the death or prior circumstances.
4. *Hostile reactions* Anger directed at others, whether justified or not.
5. *Loss of patterns of conduct* Temporary disruption of usual behaviour.
6. *Adopting traits of the deceased person* Taking on some of the mannerisms or personality characteristics of the person lost.

These reactions were deemed to be 'normal' or 'healthy', in so far as they lead to a successful resolution of the situation without harm to the individual's psychological or social 'functioning'. They are seen as the characteristics of the successful management of a crisis situation.

There is, however, a range of other potential grief reactions which at one time were deemed to be 'morbid' or 'pathological' – that is, they were seen as possibly indicative of a crisis being handled in a harmful or unsuccessful way:

1. *Postponed reaction* There is no apparent immediate change, but a reaction may surface later at an unexpected or perhaps inappropriate time.
2. *Cumulative reactions* This is where the grieving process is delayed or restricted. The negative effects will be cumulative if a further loss is experienced before the initial reaction has been dealt with.
3. *Overactivity* This refers to the grieving person making him- or herself very busy, especially in matters relating to the person (or thing) lost.
4. *Development of symptoms* Health can be affected by the stress associated with loss, but more specifically, grieving individuals may develop symptoms associated with the illness of the deceased.
5. *Stress-related illness* As mentioned above, the stress involved can lead to health problems, sometimes to quite a serious level: ulcerative colitis, asthma or psychosomatic reactions, for example.
6. *Disruption of social relationships* Grief can lead to the avoidance of people or irritation with them.

7. *Hostility* This can apply even towards people who have helped.
8. *Loss of affect* This involves the flattening of emotions and the feeling that 'nothing matters'.
9. *Disruption of patterns of interaction* Indecision, inactivity, constant need for prompting can have a significant effect on how the grieving person relates to others.
10. *Detrimental activities* People can start to behave in ways that are to their own disadvantage: extreme generosity or theft, for example.
11. *Agitated depression* Loss can produce feelings of worthlessness and bitterness.

It should be noted that these should be seen as only potentially problematic and do not automatically indicate that grieving is 'going wrong' in some way. Each can be seen as 'warning signs' of potential problems, rather than clear indicators of a failure to grieve effectively. It should also be noted that the idea of 'pathological' grieving has now been largely replaced by the less judgemental notion of 'complicated' grieving, although this term too is a contested one (see Part Four for further information about literature relating to these issues). It can be very harmful to be judgemental about how someone is responding to a loss situation, especially as we now recognise that different people grieve in different ways (see below). We therefore have to assess such situations very carefully.

From this early understanding of the crisis of bereavement, a tradition in crisis theory developed, with major steps made in the 1960s (Caplan, 1961; Langsley and Kaplan, 1968). Lindemann's ideas were generalised to other forms of loss – for example, loss of job, status, self-esteem, health, or loss through divorce. On the basis of clinical findings it was theorised that a standard pattern of grief reaction is to be found in all crises. The idea that there is in any sense a 'standard' way of grieving has now been strongly challenged (see Thompson, 2002), but, even though that reaction will be different for different people, it remains fair to say that crises are likely to provoke a grief reaction. An understanding of loss and the concomitant grief reactions is therefore a key aspect of learning about crisis theory.

Stages of crisis

In a classic work, Caplan (1961) saw crises as having three distinct phases as follows:

1. The impact stage

This initial stage is characterised by stress and confusion and a sense of disbelief. The situation seems unreal. Comments such as: 'I can't believe it's happened' or 'It hasn't sunk in yet' are not uncommon. Profound feelings of emptiness, loss and disorientation are experienced.

2. The recoil stage

This first stage is relatively short lived and quickly leads on to 'the recoil stage' which is characterised by disorganisation and intensity of emotion. This emotion can be directed outwards as anger or inwards as guilt, or indeed both simultaneously. The disorganisation common at this stage can lead to incompetence – for example, in using machinery or driving. Physical symptoms can also feature at this stage of the crisis process – for example, fatigue, headaches, stomach disorder.

3. Adjustment and adaptation

The crisis literature contains differing estimates of the timescale of the crisis process, but most fall within a four- to eight-week framework. The adjustment and adaptation stage is therefore reached in a relatively short period. It is the 'exit' stage of the crisis, as it is at this point that the success or failure of the crisis resolution will be determined. This is the stage of 'breakthrough or breakdown'. The situation is resolved to a greater or lesser extent as the available coping resources are mobilised. Breakthrough occurs when new and effective coping methods are learned or new sources of support are discovered or created. Breakdown occurs when an inappropriate or ineffective method is used, for in such circumstances this is likely to provoke a further crisis in which the coping resources will be further challenged. This third stage is the time at which skilled intervention can be crucial. It can mean the difference between breakthrough and breakdown.

While this overall three-stage framework can be a useful way of understanding crisis, it is important that it is not used in a rigid, oversimplified or uncritical way. It has to be recognised that different people will respond to crisis in different ways. The stages framework should therefore be seen as part of our understanding but certainly not the whole story. For example, we also need to consider what we have learned from stress theory and trauma theory (see Part Four for details of literature on these subjects).

The potential for growth

The worker's task within crisis intervention can therefore be seen as helping the person(s) in crisis to develop new and effective coping mechanisms. When such learning is achieved, the people concerned grow stronger as they are now better equipped to cope with the next crisis when it comes. And the next crisis surely will come, as crises, whether major or minor, are a basic part of life.

Such crises are of two basic types, situational and maturational. The latter are the 'life crises' of developmental psychology – adolescence, parenthood, the menopause, and so on. There is a certain, albeit limited, predictability associated with these crises – they follow a certain pattern or regularity (see Erikson, 1977). Situational crises, by contrast, are relatively individualised and unpredictable – they depend very much on personal circumstances.

Whatever the type of crisis, there should be an identifiable 'precipitant event', the response to which is the commencement of the crisis. The 'precipitant event' can be seen as the objective dimension, while the 'precipitant' is the subjective response to that event. The subjective dimension is primary, for an event not perceived as a crisis will not be experienced as a crisis. For example, while one person may be plunged into crisis by being involved in a road traffic accident, others may not, as they are able to take such matters in their stride – they are better equipped in terms of coping resources. Such resources consist of skills and coping strategies developed by previous personal experience, together with wider social and economic resources. Traditional crisis theory can be criticised for emphasising the former (the psychological) at the expense of the latter (the sociological), but we shall return to this point below.

Precipitating factors are important aspects of the way a crisis develops, but it is not necessary to know what precipitated the crisis. The precise details are not needed for intervention to be effective, and this is indeed consistent with a further principle of crisis intervention, that of future orientation. Here there is a link with solution-focused approaches (Myers, 2007), with their emphasis on exploring steps towards a solution (the future), rather than analysing the causes of the crisis (the past).

When a crisis is encountered, feelings of not coping are experienced and the question arises: how am I going to cope in future? The future is therefore an important dimension and crisis theory posits that intervention should consequently be future oriented. This is a significant departure from other schools of thought, such as psychodynamics and behaviourism, which focus on the significance of the past and can lead to a form of emotional paralysis characterised by constant rumination over what has happened or what has been lost. Crises often produce a tendency to dwell on past failures, whereas the positive thrust of crisis intervention seeks to concentrate on future successes by developing new coping mechanisms – and thus reintroduce hope. In simple terms, crisis theory argues that there is no point 'crying over spilled milk', and, instead, the energy generated by the crisis should be channelled positively towards the future.

This is not to say that past experiences are never significant, but rather, to emphasise that, at a time of crisis, there is more to be gained by focusing on the positive future potential, rather than analysing the past. After the crisis is over and its positive benefits have been fully exploited, there may well be much to be gained from looking back over how the situations arose and how such problems can be prevented in the future – but by focusing on such issues during the crisis, there is the danger that the positive potential will not be realised.

A key concept within the crisis theory framework is that of 'homeostasis', the ability to maintain control of our emotions and to cope with our personal circumstances. It refers to a balanced state in which everyday problems are met with, and overcome by, our usual repertoire of coping methods. In short, it is precisely a state of 'non-crisis', a psychological equilibrium. It is not necessarily a happy state, as it can be very stressful, but the point is that the balance is maintained without serious challenge to the individual. 'Homeostasis' is the traditional term, although this can be slightly misleading as it implies a static situation. The reality is that, within our normal homeostatic limits there will be considerable variation and movement: one day may be better or worse than the rest. 'Homeodynamics' would perhaps be a better term, but for now the important point to note is that we all have our 'normal' range of coping, and it is when this breaks down that a crisis can be said to be experienced. That is, when homeostasis breaks down, crisis begins. Ewing (1978) expresses this classic formulation as follows:

> The individual is continually confronted with situations that threaten to upset the consistent pattern and balance of his [sic] emotional functioning... Sometimes, however, the threatening situation is of such magnitude that it cannot be readily mastered by habitual methods of problem-solving. It is then, says Caplan, that the individual begins to experience 'crisis'. (pp. 12-13)

There is, as Ewing goes on to say, an imbalance between the perceived threat and the resources available for coping. The distorted form of crisis intervention to which we referred in the Introduction as 'crisis survival' would simply seek to restore homeostasis as soon as possible, whereas crisis intervention proper seeks to use the crisis to develop new and better ways of coping – to empower the person(s) concerned (see Chapter 8). The effect of this development is to extend and strengthen the coping repertoire, and thus reduce the risk of further crises. In this respect, crisis survival tends to produce dependency, for an inappropriately resolved crisis is likely to produce a new crisis, but leaving those concerned feeling weakened, rather than strengthened, by the initial crisis experience. Crisis intervention, by contrast, discourages dependency by teaching people how to cope, strengthening and empowering them so that their independence is promoted.

This is a significant practice implication of crisis theory and there are indeed many such implications. These will be the topic of Chapter 4 and will also be relevant to Chapters 2, 3 and 8.

Weaknesses in crisis theory

This, then is a very basic introduction to traditional crisis theory but, before moving on to examine how these ideas can be realised in practice, let us first pinpoint a number of criticisms and consider how the theory can be modified and extended to take account of them.

One significant weakness apparent in the crisis intervention approach is its relative overemphasis on 'internal' psychological coping resources and underemphasis on wider social or community resources for coping. A crisis can be an opportunity not only for developing coping skills or psychological mechanisms, but also for discovering or cultivating other sources of support or assistance within the local community or the wider social sphere – for example, a self-help group. The crisis literature does acknowledge and refer to such 'external' sources, but tends to gloss over them, as the main focus is clearly a clinical one geared towards traditional psychological issues. The wider social issues are therefore paid inadequate attention.

A more balanced crisis theory would need to develop a fuller analysis of the role and significance of wider support systems in the prevention or resolution of crises. A more sophisticated model would present the interplay of personal and social forces as well as the interplay of subjective and objective factors. This can be represented schematically as follows:

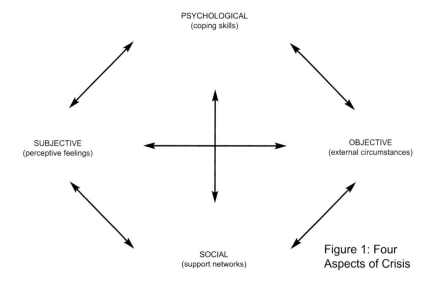

PSYCHOLOGICAL
(coping skills)

SUBJECTIVE
(perceptive feelings)

OBJECTIVE
(external circumstances)

SOCIAL
(support networks)

Figure 1: Four
Aspects of Crisis

Although there are only four elements within this matrix, it is clear that it already produces a complex set of interactions. The traditional emphasis on the psychological level alone therefore presents a rather distorted picture of the situation.

Similarly, the level of explanation of traditional crisis theory is an individual or, at best, familial one. O'Hagan (1986) was one of the first to criticise 'the pioneers' for failing to appreciate the family context of crisis situations. However, his own solution – the advocacy of a crisis intervention based on family therapy – made the same mistake, that of ignoring its own context, this time the cultural and structural aspects of the wider context. How well equipped a person is to deal with a crisis depends upon not only psychological factors, not only family dynamics, but also cultural formations and structural social divisions, such as class, race and gender (Thompson, 2006a). We shall explore these issues in more detail in Chapter 6.

The existential basis of crisis

In addition to the cultural and structural dimension neglected by the early theorists, Nira Kfir introduces a further dimension paid insufficient attention by the 'pioneers', namely the relevance of existential issues to an understanding of crisis (Seligson, 1987).

As a rule, existential issues (that is, questions about the purpose and meaning of life) are rarely addressed. Within the complacency of homeostasis we take such matters for granted and, if they do arise, they are usually dismissed by jokes about 'the meaning of life' and so on. However, at a time of crisis, such issues tend to loom large. Feelings of loneliness, emptiness and meaninglessness are characteristic of crisis as it is, in effect, an existential experience, in so far as it replaces the security of homeostasis with doubt and existential uncertainty. Seligson comments:

> In crisis, the person feels that there is no future, therefore they have no goals and hence no meaning in life. Only that person in crisis knows when the meaning of his life collapses. This is the essential existential loneliness of the crisis situation. Everything is nothing. (1987, p. 77)

Indeed, crisis theory owes much to existentialism with its emphasis on the interplay of subjective and objective factors, unpredictability and uncertainty and the need to take positive control of one's life.

Existential issues are closely linked to the notion of spirituality. Spirituality can be seen as the ways in which people come to terms with the fundamental questions of what it means to be alive, what it means to be a person and part of a wider society. For very many people religion is the basis of their spirituality; it is where they find at least some of the answers to these questions (Moss, 2005). For very many others, their spirituality lies outside the religious sphere – that is, they have other, non-religious ways of addressing the questions. However, whether rooted in religion or not, spirituality can be seen as a key aspect of how we cope with life's challenges.

Bearing this in mind we can see that some crises may be spiritual crises – that is, the individual(s) concerned may experience a breakdown in their understanding of what their life is all about and may therefore feel very vulnerable and 'all at sea'. Crises associated with major loss or trauma can be especially significant in this regard, as they can result in situations where people feel they no longer know who they are or how and where they fit into the world.

Existentialism stresses the importance of choices, of the decisions we make and the consequences which flow from these, both in personal and social terms, individual and collective. Such decisions are characterised by risk and contingency, and so the potential for losing control and entering crisis is an everpresent one and therefore something we need to learn to come to terms with. Over 50 years ago, Rollo May, an existentialist psychotherapist recognised that: 'Existentialism is an attitude which accepts [wo]man as always becoming, which means potentially in crisis' (May *et al.*, 1958, p. 86).

While existentialism is an influential school of thought in counselling and psychotherapy (van Deurzen and Arnold-Baker, 2005), its status and influence in the other helping professions is of a much lower order. However, to maximise our understanding of crises and appropriate interventions, a fuller understanding of the existential aspects should be high on the agenda.

Traditional crisis theory is premised on the 'ego psychology' approach of writers such as Erikson (1977), but what I hope is now clear is that such a theoretical basis is inadequate and needs to be extended in a number of ways. Over twenty years ago O'Hagan (1986) recognised some of the weaknesses, castigated the 'pioneers' for their narrow, psychiatric focus and proposed family systems theory as an improvement. However, as mentioned earlier, this did not go far enough. It neglected the cultural, structural and existential dimensions, all of which have significant and far-reaching implications for theory, practice and policy. It was also based on an approach known as 'systems theory' which can be criticised, from an existentialist point of view, for being dehumanising and not well suited to the very human nature of crisis (Thompson, 1992).

The flaws apparent within crisis theory are major ones but, having acknowledged this, we should beware the danger of 'throwing the baby out with the bath water', by rejecting crisis intervention as an inappropriate or outmoded approach to dealing with people in distress.

Much work needs to be done to strengthen the theoretical basis of crisis work so that it can provide a more adequate knowledge base to guide practice. Chapters 7 and 8 make a small contribution to this. However, what also needs to be achieved – and here I am in agreement with O'Hagan – is the development of practice skills, the actual 'nuts and bolts' of dealing effectively and constructively with people experiencing disabling crises. The development of theory is therefore not an end in itself, but rather a means to an end. That end is the establishment of high-quality professional practice, based on the reflective use of crisis intervention principles.

Conclusion

To conclude this introductory chapter on the theory base of crisis intervention, let me summarise, in diagram form, the theoretical developments I see as necessary for the revitalisation of crisis intervention as a major approach to helping people who are experiencing significant difficulties.

Old	New
Psychology	Psychology and sociology
Adjustment	Empowerment
Consensus	Conflict
Family context	Social-structural context:
	class
	race / ethnicity
	gender
	age and so on
Focus on individual	Holistic focus (including individual/family)
Internal	Internal and external
No specific philosophical basis	Existentialist basis
Pathological	Psychosocial
Personal resources	Personal and social resources

Figure 2. Crisis Theory

What I seek to do, therefore, is to build upon the sound foundations of early crisis theory but, in doing so, discard those aspects which are inappropriate to modern-day professional practice and replace them with more relevant and less restricted concepts, which thus gives us a much stronger framework for intervention.

Points to ponder

> ➤ How might you recognise whether someone is in crisis (rather than just distressed)?
> ➤ Why do you think experiencing a major loss so often leads to a crisis?
> ➤ Why do you think it is important not simply to help people return to their pre-crisis state?

Chapter 2
The Positive Dimension of Crisis

Introduction

A crisis is a turning point, a time of decision in which a prior state of equilibrium has been disturbed. The result of this can be either positive or negative – our capacity to cope with future problems, stresses and crises can be enhanced or diminished.

As Everstine and Everstine (2006) point out, the Chinese character representing 'crisis' means both opportunity and danger. This captures well the positive potential of crisis together with the significant risk of harm, whether this be physical, emotional or social. The intervention of the crisis worker can be crucial in determining which way the outcome of the crisis falls – positive or negative.

The crisis response

The crisis situation is likely to produce a biological stress response as the 'fight or flight' mechanism is activated. The body responds by releasing adrenaline and thereby producing extra energy which in turn is likely to lead to a higher level of motivation. The physical concomitants of crisis are many: higher pulse rate, dry mouth, 'butterflies' sensation and so on. These are the bodily manifestations of feelings of anxiety, threat or loss.

However, when we consider the bodily response to feelings of joy, exhilaration or celebration, we can detect strong, if not exact, parallels with the stress response. The body responds to both stress and excitement in basically the same way – that is, by entering a 'state of arousal'. It is this state of arousal that the crisis worker can use to the full in attempting to realise a positive outcome from the crisis by exploiting the energy and motivation generated. From an ethical point of view we should note that it is a matter of exploiting the opportunities offered by the crisis situation to help the person(s) in crisis benefit from the growth potential afforded, rather than to exploit the person(s) concerned in order to manipulate them into doing what we want them to do.

This state of arousal is known in acting circles as the 'buzz', that state of nervous excitement which can either inhibit or inspire. Drama teaching involves learning to control this 'buzz' and use it as a positive tool. Similarly, assertiveness training involves attempting to harness the strong feelings produced by situations of conflict or potential confrontation and use them in a positive and constructive way (indeed, assertiveness is an important basis of crisis intervention – see below).

At a biological, bodily level, the sensations experienced in extreme situations are the same, regardless of whether it is a positive or negative extreme. It is at the psychological, rather than the physical, level that we distinguish between the two extremes, between joy and fear. The body's response is a recognition of an unusual, extraordinary situation or, to use the jargon, a breakdown of homeostasis. In this sense, an extreme situation of joy can be a crisis, with both danger and opportunity present. An example of how such a crisis can 'go wrong' is that of the 'spend, spend, spend' problems of some football pools or lottery winners, arising from the breakdown of their normal coping mechanisms and psychologically important sense of equilibrium (there is a significant overlap here with Durkheim's concept of 'anomie' or 'normlessness' where people can feel all at sea – Durkheim, 1952).

The physical sensations are the objective dimension, but we must also acknowledge the subjective dimension – the interpretation of such sensations, the meanings we attach to them. How we interpret these will depend very much on the circumstances of their occurrence in relation to the goals and values we have adopted (in part a reflection of our cultural context and our 'social location' in terms of such social structures as class, race, gender, age and so on). And this is where the positive use of crisis comes to the fore, as it is possible for us to alter our goals or values if the circumstances dictate. This is known as 'cognitive restructuring' and is a common way of coping with stress. For example, if I fail an exam or fail to get a job I applied for, one way of coping with the negative feelings is to change direction, to develop a different ambition or aspiration.

The task of the crisis worker may therefore be to help the person(s) in crisis review or renegotiate certain aspects of their thoughts, feelings or intentions. This, of course, is not as simple as it may initially sound, but the positive potential is none the less there. In the same way that there is nothing inherently good or bad about the bodily response to crisis – it is 'neutral' – there is nothing inherently good or bad about the psychological response to the situation – it all depends on how we deal with it. Crisis intervention – and this is the crux – is geared towards helping people maximise the positive potential by dealing effectively with the 'crisis matrix', the various aspects of the crisis situation, and thus exploiting the learning opportunities generated.

Within crisis theory, the term 'crisis' is not to be equated with the common-sense usage in the sense of a 'disaster', as this necessarily entails a negative conclusion. A crisis, in this technical sense, is potentially negative or positive and

I shall discuss below some of the ways in which the balance can be tilted towards the positive.

To illustrate this further, let us consider the different levels of coping and a 'chart' of how these can be affected by crisis – see Figure 3 below.

Levels of coping

Each of us has a characteristic 'level of functioning' in terms of our ability to – deal with the range of problems we encounter in our day-to-day circumstances. This 'normal' level of functioning is that of homeostasis. Crisis occurs, by definition, when this homeostatic level of equilibrium is upset. Equilibrium will eventually be restored, but it may be at a different level. This new level could be lower, in which case the crisis can be seen to have attacked and reduced our coping abilities. For example, a court appearance may leave someone with little or no pride or confidence, and therefore that person is less well equipped to deal with other problems and challenges as and when they arise. The same precipitant event, a court appearance, may, by contrast, be a significant turning point in a positive way. It may give a strong determination to steer clear of potential law breaking and take a more controlled, less aimless, approach to one's life and thus produce more effective coping skills and a higher level of functioning.

The outcome level is therefore variable, depending upon the response of the person(s) in crisis and, where applicable, the crisis worker(s). These different levels can be represented diagrammatically as follows:

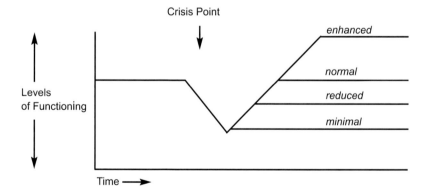

Figure 3: Levels
of Functioning,
Based on Hill, 1965

Crisis inevitably produces a lowering of coping ability on a temporary basis as we pass through the impact and recoil phases. However, to what level it returns in the exit phase is not predictable, as it depends so much on the actions of those involved.

In order to ensure, as far as possible, that the outcome is a beneficial one in terms of an enhanced level of functioning, steps must be taken to minimise the danger element and concentrate on the opportunity element (although it has to be recognised that the precipitant event may be anything but positive – for example the death of a loved one, but the ensuing crisis may have positive implications in terms of enhancing our future ability to cope. See Part Four for details of literature relating to the notion of 'transformational grief'). This is the basis of crisis intervention and can be achieved in a number of ways, for example:

1. By mobilising appropriate support system resources – for example, through advocacy.
2. Through rapport and positive interest, offering the person(s) in crisis a degree of calming reassurance and a temporary prop to their self-esteem and confidence. It should not be underestimated how significant such a relatively simple step can be.
3. By facilitating the learning of new and more effectice coping mechanisms – for example, through solution-focused approaches (Greene *et al.*, 2008; Myers, 2007) or involvement in groupwork (Doel, 2005; Everly *et al.*, 2008).

These issues will be addressed more fully in Chapter 4, but it is worth noting at this stage that such forms of intervention play a significant role in the positive use of crisis. This is to be distinguished, as indeed it was earlier, from 'crisis survival' which seeks to restore homeostasis as quickly as possible, rather than as constructively as possible.

A further point which needs to be emphasised is that we should not confuse the positive use of crisis with a strategy of provoking crisis as part of one's efforts to help. It should be remembered that crisis represents not only opportunity but also danger. Deliberately provoking a crisis, albeit in a well-intentioned way as part of an overall strategy, may none the less result in considerable harm to vulnerable people. The ethics of such an approach are very questionable indeed. Crisis intervention entails capitalising on crises – making the best of a bad situation, as it were – but this is very different from causing a crisis. This point has often been misunderstood and crisis intervention has therefore attracted inappropriate and inaccurate criticism at times.

Crisis theory and other approaches to helping

One of the great strengths of crisis theory is that it can quite easily be combined with other approaches to helping. Consider the following examples:

- *Counselling* Given the time-limited nature of a crisis, a long-term counselling approach is unlikely to be appropriate. However, at a time of crisis, short-term intensive counselling can prove very beneficial as the person in crisis is much more likely to be open to making the needed changes to their life than would be the case while they are settled in the relative security of homeostasis.
- *Cognitive behavioural work* The foundation of this approach is the idea that where behaviour needs to change for some reason (because it is causing problems or distress, for example), then it is the underlying belief(s) leading to the behaviour that needs to change. At a time of crisis there is likely to be more commitment to changing underlying beliefs, more motivation to trying out new ideas or approaches to situations.
- *Task-centred practice* This involves establishing (i) where you are now; (ii) where you want to be; and (iii) what steps need to be taken to move from (i) (a problematic, unacceptable situation) to (ii) (a less problematic, acceptable situation). These steps are then defined in terms of tasks to be achieved. Much of this depends on motivation and, at a time of crisis, motivation to bring about change is likely to be higher than at other times.
- *Solution-focused approaches* This involves focusing on strengths and, in particular, identifying situations when the problem in question does not apply (for example, if someone has panic attacks, what are the situations when he or she does not panic? How can the lessons from this then be applied to those situations where panic occurs?). This is very consistent with the emphasis on positive potential in crisis intervention.
- *Advocacy* People in crisis are, by definition, struggling to cope. At such times they may find it difficult to stand up for their rights and to avoid exploitation or injustice. They may therefore need the support of an advocate to help them through this difficult period. An advocate drawing on principles of crisis intervention is likely to act directly as an advocate to begin with, but then to support the individual concerned to develop self-advocacy so that they are able to use the positive potential of the crisis to learn new skills and develop new personal resources.
- *Groupwork* In the limited timeframe relating to crisis work it can be difficult to coordinate involvement in groupwork. However, where it is possible, it can be extremely helpful and empowering, as the person concerned can use the support of the group as an emotional and practical resource as well as a forum for developing new ways of coping.

This is not intended as an exhaustive list. Rather, it is to be seen as illustrative of the possible linkages of different approaches. It is the task of the critically reflective practitioner to work in partnership to determine what combination of methods will be most helpful in the particular circumstances (see Chapter 3 for a discussion of assessment).

A further dimension of theory which is of very direct and significant relevance to crisis intervention is that of systematic practice (Thompson, 2009a; 2009b). The basic idea behind systematic practice is that there should be clarity about what the helper and helped – working in partnership – are trying to achieve, how they are planning to achieve it and how they will know they have achieved it (that is, what success will look like). This type of structured (but not rigid) framework with a clear focus can be very helpful in general in creating a sense of order and security that people can find very helpful, but when someone is in crisis and feeling all at sea, this clarity and focus can be extremely helpful for them. It is therefore important to give careful consideration to using crisis intervention in tandem with systematic practice.

Systematic practice is characterised by goal setting. From the beginning of our intervention, goal setting will be important in order to give a framework to the work being done. One of the characteristics of crisis is a feeling of loss of control, a lack of structure and therefore a sense of meaninglessness and alienation. Consequently, it is important to re-establish the parameters, to create a new and meaningful framework. Goal setting is an important way of helping to build a supportive structured framework. Such a framework can offer considerable reassurance at a time when they could very much benefit from it.

Goal setting is based on positive achievement and should be a process worked out in partnership. It is neither ethical nor helpful for the worker simply to impose his or her own goals (indeed it can be positively harmful to do so) as the aim is not just to help the client survive the crisis, but rather to learn from this crisis in order to cope better with future demands and potential and actual crises. There is also the issue of the potential for abuse of the power the worker has over the client who is vulnerable by virtue of his or her crisis state, as mentioned earlier. It is therefore vital to work with the client in both establishing and working towards goals, although it should be noted that the pressure of a crisis can make it a strong temptation to work at your own pace and in your own direction. This is clearly a temptation that needs to be resisted.

In general, it needs to be emphasised that goals should be short term and incremental. In the intense emotional 'heat' of a crisis, the timescale is very telescoped, and so long-term goals are likely to have little meaning in such situations. Also, it is important for people in crisis to develop a sense of 'progress', a sense that they are gradually regaining their equilibrium. The incremental nature of goal setting is therefore highly appropriate to this task of instilling a sense of progress. The hope that this can bring can be very important indeed.

It is far better to have a series of short-term goals rather than one major long-term goal, although there is, of course, always the one major long-term aim, that of enhancing the client's problem-solving and coping methods.

In setting goals, it should be remembered that these should be reasonably easy to achieve. This is for two reasons:

1. Nothing succeeds like success. Success in relation to one goal enhances the chance of success in achieving subsequent goals.
2. Setting a goal which is too difficult or unrealistic is to set someone up to fail.

Goal setting, within a framework of systematic practice can therefore clearly be seen to offer significant benefits when it comes to helping people in crisis.

Conclusion

Crisis, by its very nature, can be seen to raise considerable potential for positive change. In a sense, a crisis reshuffles the pack, and thus, with a mixture of careful handling and good luck, a much better hand can be dealt.

Crisis is potentially both very destructive and very constructive. It can seriously undermine, on a long-term basis, our 'level of functioning' in terms of coping mechanisms or it can lead to a much higher and more rewarding level of coping by exploiting the excellent learning and development opportunities afforded by the breakdown of homeostatic equilibrium. The crisis worker can be a major figure in determining which way the situation goes. The aim therefore is not simply to minimise the harm of a crisis, to 'cut losses', but rather to maximise the positive potential of crisis.

By examining the biological basis of the feelings experienced in crisis, it was seen that there is little or no difference in the physical sensations of extreme joy or extreme fear or anxiety. Thus, with some degree of training and positive support, as in assertiveness training, this physical 'buzz' can be used as a source of energy and motivation rather than inhibition and disincentive. Again, the role of the crisis worker can be crucial in positively harnessing this nervous energy. In doing so, weakness is turned into strength, and considerable potential harm becomes a very powerful source of positive and constructive energy.

We have also seen that the use of crisis theory does not necessarily exclude the use of other approaches or methods. Indeed, a combination of methods within the context of critically reflective practice can be very effective indeed. One of the points to be made more fully in Chapter 4 is that one of the clear strengths of crisis intervention as a method of helping is that it does not preclude the use of other approaches. It offers great flexibility in terms of the repertoire of methods used within a crisis intervention framework.

Crisis theory is premised on the value of concentrating on the positive, and steadily building up an increased level of coping skills and confidence. We have noted that this is facilitated by the key process of short-term, incremental goal setting.

The two theoretical perspectives, crisis intervention and systematic practice, are highly compatible, in that they both place great emphasis on making a virtue of concentrating on the positive and using it as both a tool and a principle of intervention.

The focus within this chapter on the positive dimension of crisis provides a very suitable backdrop for an examination of the actual practice of crisis intervention. We are therefore now ready to proceed to a consideration of 'doing crisis work', and that is what Part Two is all about.

The next chapter focuses on issues relating to assessing crisis situations and this sets the scene for Chapter 4 which tackles the central issues of practising crisis intervention, the 'nuts and bolts' of practice.

Points to ponder

> ➢ What do you see as the difference between crisis survival and crisis intervention?
> ➢ In what ways might it be possible to capitalise on the energy and motivation generated by the crisis?
> ➢ What other helping approaches do you currently use in your work that could be combined with a crisis intervention approach?

Introduction

While Part One laid the foundations by discussing the main elements of the theory base, Part Two now seeks to build on that by exploring some of the practice implications of drawing on the insights of crisis theory. The overall aim is to show how crisis theory is not only interesting as a way of understanding what happens to people at key times in their life, but also useful as a guide to practice. The idea is not to provide a simple set of formulas to follow, as if theory can be directly applied to practice in a straightforward way. Rather, it is a case of providing a discussion that should cast a great deal of light on crisis situations and our efforts to capitalise on them – a discussion that should provide a solid foundation for critically reflective practice (Thompson and Thompson, 2008a).

Part Two has four chapters, covering in turn: assessment; intervention; case examples; and some of the main implications of working within a crisis intervention framework. Together these provide a helpful basis for developing a good working knowledge of crisis intervention and how it can be used in a variety of settings across the helping professions.

Chapter 3
Assessment

Introduction

High-quality professional practice relies on a good assessment, the gathering of information to provide a helpful picture of the key issues, the problems to be addressed and the strengths to be drawn upon. Making an assessment of a situation in which people are hurt, angry, distressed or grieving is always difficult. It is not possible to apply straightforward, objective or 'scientific' criteria or methodology. A rigid approach is not only unlikely to succeed, but may actually make the situation much worse by alienating or further distressing the client(s).

This much is true of all assessment, but is particularly the case in crisis work. In crisis, clients are especially vulnerable and therefore good assessment work is vital to ensure that help is maximised and harm minimised. But what are the principles of assessment that apply particularly to crisis intervention? An exploration of these principles, the skills required and the pitfalls to avoid, is precisely what we shall now undertake.

Principles of crisis assessment

In order to give a picture of what is involved in high-quality crisis assessment I shall now outline what I see as eight important principles that should underpin assessment.

1. Early assessment is crucial

As crises are time limited, it is extremely important to ensure that the assessment process is begun early. The exit phase of the crisis is when new solutions are found and, of course, it is at this point that unhelpful or counterproductive solutions may be adopted. It is therefore of major importance that an assessment and plan of intervention have been developed before the client(s) get too far into the exit phase. Delaying assessment is likely to result in 'missing the boat', and so the luxury of 'well, let's see how it goes' cannot be afforded in crisis work.

2. Both the subjective and the objective dimensions must be included

It is not only the 'objective', external circumstances which contribute to a crisis situation, but also the subjective issues of emotional response, perception and interpretation. The assessment task is therefore twofold. On the one hand, the professional helper needs to know what has happened, what actions or events have played a part in producing a state of disequilibrium. On the other hand (and this is perhaps the more difficult task), the helper also needs to understand, as far as possible, the subjective issues – for example, the coping methods previously used, the emotional impact and overall personal significance of what has happened, the attitude towards future development and direction and so on.

The key technical term here is 'the precipitant'. We need to know not only the precipitant event – that is, the objective 'trigger(s)' – but also the personal psychological response which identifies the situation as a crisis. The concept of 'precipitant' therefore encompasses both objective and subjective dimensions, as a useful assessment must take account of both of these aspects (see Thompson, 2010, for a discussion of the 'dialectic of subjectivity and objectivity' – that is, the process through which subjective and objective aspects interact and influence each other).

3. Assessment should not have a narrow, psychological focus

The traditional approach to crisis intervention, as we saw in Chapter 1, is a rather narrow one which focuses on psychological coping strengths. Wider social issues are mentioned, but are not developed or fully integrated into the approach. In order to overcome this traditional weakness, good assessment must take account of two sets of wider, social factors:

a) Social resources for coping

Family, friends, neighbours, welfare organisations, self-help groups and so on must be seen as part of what can be called 'the coping matrix' – that is, the web of factors that combine to shape how pressures are dealt with.

b) Social location

Social divisions such as class, race and gender are also significant parts of the coping matrix. One's location in society can be plotted along these axes, and this social location (Thompson, 2011a) will give important clues as to the pressures faced by the client(s) – for example, economic pressures, racism, sexism – and also potential sources of support, such as trade unions, black support organisations, women's groups and so on.

There is, however, a conflict here between a perceived shortage of time and the breadth of factors to be considered. It therefore needs to be recognised that pragmatic considerations of time will inevitably limit the breadth of the assessment to a certain extent. However, this should not be used as an excuse for concentrating only on the traditional, psychological factors. Crisis intervention is a psychosocial approach, and so assessment should encompass both psychological and sociological issues.

4. Focus on the positive

An assessment should not simply be a list of problems, worries or weaknesses. It is also necessary to identify areas of strength, as the plan of intervention will seek to draw attention to these areas and build on them as a key part of the therapeutic process (see Saleebey, 2008, for a discussion of the importance of what has come to be known as 'the strengths perspective').

Identifying areas in which the client is coping well is significant for a number of reasons:

a) It gives a baseline from which to build further new coping methods.

b) It helps to give client and professional helper a degree of confidence.

c) It gives opportunities for the helper to reinforce those coping skills (see Chapter 2) and immediately begin work on constructing a positive attitude and frame of reference.

Identifying strengths can be a difficult task for those workers who are schooled and experienced in more traditional problem-solving approaches in which the focus is clearly on an analysis of the negative elements with little reference to the positives.

Identifying and reinforcing strong points needs to be handled carefully and sensitively, as it may give an impression that we are uninterested in the problems and have an unrealistically rosy picture of the situation. We shall return to this point below under the heading of 'skills required'.

5. Medicalisation should be avoided

The temptation to simplify a complex psychosocial situation by applying a medical label is a temptation to be strongly resisted.

In crisis, a person's behaviour may be bizarre, unpredictable or self-destructive; sometimes behaviour may appear quite 'insane'. However, such behaviour must be seen in context, the context of a crisis in which usual coping mechanisms have broken down and left the person concerned feeling helpless and at a loss. We should be careful not to confuse such stress responses with mental disorder. Such medicalisation (or 'psychiatrisation') merely distorts a complex and painful reality with social and psychological dimensions into a physiologically based disease process. If the focus is on an assumed 'mental illness', key factors relating to the crisis matrix may be missed, translated into 'symptoms' or simply not spotted because the professionals involved were not sufficiently attuned to crisis issues (see Case B in Chapter 5).

Reliance on a medical diagnosis is therefore the easy way out, but, as we know, taking the easy way out is rarely the best way forward and is often counterproductive in the long run.

In formulating an assessment, strange behaviour (for example, a recently bereaved widow acting as if her husband is still with her) should be interpreted as quite probably a crisis response rather than necessarily the symptom of a mental disorder. It is important to note that her acting in this way would be seen, from a crisis theory point of view, as a means of coping with her loss, part of a process of grieving and therefore a solution rather than a problem. We should be careful not to try to take away this coping method until she is ready to take on a better or more effective way of coping. In other words, we should not take away her metaphorical crutch until she has been helped sufficiently to walk without its assistance. Assessment should take account of such issues.

6. Identifying the problem focus

Clients in crisis are often not in a position to articulate their problems, and so some degree of 'detective work', in the form of careful and sensitive questioning, is usually needed to clarify the focus of the problem. For example, the client may blame the 'last straw', the final event or action which ultimately provoked the crisis, whereas other factors, subjective and/or objective, may have been just as significant, if not more so. A person in crisis is likely to be confused and distraught and therefore not the best judge of the situation.

However, we need to be careful here and strike a balance. Crisis workers need to avoid taking over, invading their clients' territories and imposing their own definition of the situation. Where the views of helper and client differ, such disagreement must be discussed and as much agreement as possible reached. The reason for this is that crisis intervention is geared towards self-direction and empowerment. It is not possible to empower someone to follow a plan of action with which he or she disagrees. Only coercion, manipulation or persuasion can do this, and none of these amounts to empowerment.

Clarity about the problem focus is also an important basis for systematic practice, as discussed earlier. If we are not clear what the problem is, we are going to struggle to help people find solutions to it.

7. Clear plans need to be formulated

The basic aim of assessment is to accumulate sufficient and appropriate information to produce a workable plan of intervention – that is, an outline of what needs to be done and how it can and should be done.

Crisis is a time characterised by confusion, lack of structure and lack of control. In view of this scenario, it is therefore important that plans should be clear and easily understood. They should not be vague and woolly or ambiguous. Sharing such plans with a person in crisis will only add to the sense of being out of control and thus raise barriers to positive intervention. Clear, well-formulated, explicit plans can, on the contrary, help to re-establish control, order and meaning and thus prevent panic and deterioration. Sharing clear plans with a person in crisis therefore facilitates positive intervention and gets the whole process off to a beneficial and constructive start.

However, we should be careful not to confuse clear plans with rigid plans. In a crisis there are many unpredictable variables, and therefore plans need to be flexible and subject to easy review. There is a major difference between being clear about what you intend to do and being dogged or rigid about it. The former may include a willingness to change plans as and when circumstances dictate, whereas the latter certainly does not.

8. A balanced approach to risk assessment is needed

Crisis necessarily involves risk for all concerned for, as we have seen, crisis is precisely a time when contingency is to the fore, when uncertainty and instability are very much in evidence.

This has three major implications for crisis workers:

a) The degree of risk to clients, their families, associates and so on needs to be carefully and thoroughly assessed. Child protection and statutory mental health duties are examples of work where such risk analysis can be crucial.

b) The risk faced by the worker also needs to be given due attention. Violence to professional helpers is not unheard of, and the highly charged atmosphere of crisis may make such violence all the more possible. Crisis workers should therefore make every effort to safeguard themselves from harm – for example, by doing certain visits accompanied. Being attacked by a client in crisis does the crisis worker no good, and the likely repercussions of such an attack will not do the client any favours either.

c) Taking informed and well thought-out risks is an essential part of crisis intervention, and so the worker should be ready and willing to take appropriate risks as and when the circumstances dictate. Maximising the positive potential of a crisis necessarily involves some degree of gambling. A crisis worker who is not prepared to take risks or is ill-equipped to make informed judgments about risk is highly unlikely to be an effective crisis worker.

In sum, risk is integral to crisis intervention, and it is therefore important for crisis workers to build up the skills of risk analysis: a sensitivity to the balance between overcaution on the one hand and reckless risk taking on the other. Allied to this is the ability to cope with the intense contingency of the minefield of risks crisis workers face.

These, then, are what I see as the fundamental principles of crisis assessment, although I am by no means arguing that this is an exhaustive list. It is recognised that there are many other areas of assessment which could usefully be explored, but it is beyond the scope of this text to take this matter any further. It is to be hoped that I have at least provided a starting point from which people can launch themselves into developing high-quality crisis assessment.

These principles as outlined are, of course, an important part of the process of assessment, but they are clearly not the only part. A second part, and one which has received relatively little attention, is that of skills development. Assessment in general is a skill-based activity, but crisis assessment needs to be especially skilful and relies on a particular set of skills. It is to an examination of such issues that we now turn.

Crisis assessment skills

There are various skills that underpin crisis intervention. Here I am going to focus on what I consider to be eight key skills.

1. Listening skills

The ability to listen effectively is a much valued one in the helping professions in general, and not just in crisis work. However, successful crisis intervention has to be based on effective listening, and yet the characteristics of a crisis situation – panic, high levels of emotion, possible physical danger, for example – can act as significant barriers to listening. Hearing what the client is trying to say can be prevented or obstructed in a number of ways, for example:

a) Anxiety or fear on the helper's part can get in the way. The helper's own personal agenda may overrule the client's agenda. This may particularly be the case, where power and/or conflict are significant issues – for example, where a child protection worker is dealing with a case of child abuse and is considering removing the child(ren).

b) The interference of others who are also responding to the crisis – for example, friends, relatives or people from other agencies, may make it difficult for the crisis worker to get the time and space to listen well. The good intentions and/or panic of others may therefore make the task of listening all the more difficult. However, it is also important to listen to what they have to say, as they too are part of the 'crisis matrix', the wider crisis situation.

c) Preconceptions can also be a hindrance. For example, when dealing with someone diagnosed as mentally ill, the worker may interpret valid thoughts, feelings and comments as 'symptomatic' of mental disorder (see principle number 5 above). Similarly, sexist, racist or other discriminatory stereotypes may prevent helpers from hearing what is actually being said.

One of the key skills of listening, therefore, is to remove as many barriers to communication as possible and thereby ensure that an appropriate atmosphere is created. In short, the worker needs to be able to make the time and space needed to listen. A major part of listening is allowing the client(s) to talk by doing whatever is possible to make this easy for them.

Furthermore, it should be remembered that 'listening' can also be used metaphorically to refer to taking on board nonverbal forms of communication (Mehrabian, 2007). Posture, gesture, touch and so on are significant dimensions of communication and, as we know, verbal and nonverbal communications can contradict each other (Thompson, 2009c). It is necessary for crisis workers to 'listen' to both verbal and nonverbal messages and be sensitive to the extent to which they reinforce or contradict each other.

2. Reflecting feelings

By using reflection in a simple, non-judgmental and unbiased way, the helper conveys to those in crisis that he or she is trying to understand how they feel. Good reflection involves sensing not only what the client says, but also how he or she says it.

By 'checking back' with the client in this way, the crisis worker achieves a number of things:

a) Concern for the client is expressed, and this is therapeutic in general terms, while also helping to 'lubricate' the interactions of the assessment process.

b) It limits opportunities for misunderstanding. If a worker reflects a feeling inaccurately or inappropriately, the misunderstanding is exposed and can be rectified. As the crisis assessment process needs to be a speedy one, built-in mechanisms for correcting misunderstandings are particularly valuable.

c) It humanises what can, at its worst, be a matter-of-fact process of gathering information. It begins the process of 'engaging' the client(s) and thus prepares the ground for the intervention stage proper.

Successful reflection of feelings is a delicate and sensitive skill which needs to be nurtured and developed over time.

An example of this skill in practice would be where, in response to a remark made in a tone of voice which suggests anger, the helper makes a comment along the lines of: 'You seem to be quite angry. Do you want to talk about what's bothering you?'

This type of response both shows empathy with the client and feeds back important information. For example, the client may not have realised he or she was expressing anger, as is often the case when emotions 'creep in' to our communications without our fully realising that this is happening.

Of course, we should also not forget the reflection of feelings nonverbally. The crisis worker needs to be able to reflect feelings through not only words, but also facial expressions, posture, physical distance, touch and so on. Touch can be particularly effective, but a note of caution is called for. Touch is a form of communication, and so it can easily be misinterpreted. We therefore need to be very clear about the message touch is conveying and that this is supported or confirmed verbally. Touch can be either very supportive or an oppressive invasion of personal space. If construed as the latter, a lot of harm can be done. Where the issue arises between a male helper and a female client, the question of sexual harassment can easily arise. This is a very real issue and a great cause for concern; it should not be dismissed or trivialised (Thompson, 2000b). I would therefore counsel caution by advising that touch be used selectively and sensitively.

3. Reinforcing coping skills

As was emphasised in Chapter 2, reinforcement of positives is a key aspect of crisis intervention. It forms a significant part of the intervention stage proper (see Chapter 4), but is also a fundamental component of the assessment process.

For a professional helper dealing with a client who is experiencing a crisis, one of the primary aims is to facilitate the learning of new techniques in coping. In order for the client to learn these skills, it is helpful for current skills, however minimal these may be in some cases, to be reinforced. For example, a new client expresses the following problem: 'Meeting people and making conversation with them is very difficult for me.'

The helper's response may well be: 'If that is so, then I think you have done really well to come here today and talk so openly about your feelings.'

With imagination, thought and practice, the skill of recognising opportunities to give positive reinforcement can be developed and put to very effective use.

Even in the most extreme of crisis situations it is likely that some areas of coping remain relatively unaffected and can be capitalised upon. Recognising these, and thus reinforcing them, is an assessment task.

In carrying out an assessment of a crisis situation, reinforcing coping skills can be helpful in the following ways:

a) It identifies the client's strengths.

b) It gives an indication of how responsive he or she is to a positive approach.

c) It may reveal other significant aspects of the crisis matrix.

d) It helps to 'engage' the client and thus bridge the gap between the assessment stage and the intervention stage (although it should be noted that the two can never be entirely separated anyway, as each implies elements of the other).

e) It encourages the client to share feelings and information.

Reinforcing coping skills is therefore part and parcel of assessment, but is itself a skill which needs to be developed. It requires the ability to:

a) recognise positives, even in an overwhelmingly negative situation;

b) reinforce these positives in a non-patronising and non-trivial way;

c) persuade the client to accept positives in a situation which is characterised by so many negatives.

As one might expect, developing this sort of skill is not easy, but it is none the less an important part of crisis assessment.

4. Information gathering

In order to formulate a plan of intervention, it is necessary to obtain relevant and accurate information. As people in crisis are vulnerable and relatively powerless (and the worker very powerful), breaches of civil liberties can easily occur through overintrusiveness. In view of this, the guiding principle of information gathering should be to obtain the minimum information necessary rather than the maximum information available. Having said this, it is recognised that knowing what is the minimum – that is, knowing where to stop, is not as easy as it may sound. It has to be based on skill, experience and judgment. Relying on the traditional notion of gathering as much information as possible is not appropriate to crisis intervention.

In addition to the civil liberties aspect, excessive probing or an overzealous seeking of information slows down what needs to be quite a rapid process and also it risks alienating the client(s). Information gathering should therefore be non-provocative, and the skills necessary to ensure this should be practised and developed. Below I offer some guidelines as to how to move towards achieving this:

a) Much information can be gained indirectly by 'ventilation'. That is, by creating for clients the right atmosphere to express their feelings, many relevant facts about the situation will emerge spontaneously without the need for direct questioning.

b) Crisis is a time when people are more open to any help offered and more likely to ask for help (Ewing, 1978, p. 13). It is therefore possible to elicit information about both the subjective and objective dimensions in a non-provocative, non-probing way simply by explaining what you need to know in order to be able to help. The information then needs to be clearly linked to the plan of action. This simple technique is important because it:

i)   Focuses information and interaction. In a pressurised crisis situation, unfocused assessment is counterproductive.

ii) Gives opportunities for positive reinforcement, as it links information/assessment to strategy/intervention.

iii) By explaining what information is needed and why, the worker confirms that the process is a shared one in which the worker takes away the information and comes back with 'the answer'.

c) As was emphasised in Chapter 1, the traditional focus of crisis intervention is the individual. If we widen our focus to take in 'significant others' who are part of the crisis matrix, the necessary information can be gathered from a variety of sources and thus takes some of the pressure of 'probing' off the main characters in the crisis drama.

5. Calming and being calm

Crisis produces considerable emotion and nervous energy which often spills over into panic, aggression or even violence. A certain amount of giving vent to anger is of course helpful and constructive, but beyond a certain point it becomes counterproductive and a barrier to progress.

Given that a crisis usually involves more than one person, too much tension and conflict can heighten ill-feeling and thus stand in the way of developing a positive and constructive approach. Some degree of control is therefore needed. The crisis worker needs to provide this control in three ways:

a) To be able to calm the individual(s) concerned and help them to relax. Various techniques are available for this – for example, through the effective use of body language.

b) To be able to mediate competently and successfully between people in conflict. Sometimes such conflict is the cause of the crisis (for example, marital violence); sometimes it is the result of the crisis (for example, the discovery that a child has been arrested for theft). Whichever applies, the crisis worker none the less has to be able to manage the situation sufficiently well to allow progress to be made.

c) To be able to manage our own feelings for, as we shall see below, one of the dangers of crisis work is that it plunges the worker into a crisis of his or her own. It is therefore necessary to develop skills required to deal with one's own emotional situation. This is part of the recognition of the importance of emotional intelligence – the ability to (i) 'read' other people's emotions and respond appropriately; and (ii) be aware of, and able to deal constructively with, our own feelings.

The skills of calming and remaining calm are therefore vitally important for doing effective crisis work. This is particularly the case in the assessment stage, partly because the crisis participants are usually still in the early stages of crisis and are therefore particularly vulnerable, and partly because clear intervention plans cannot be formulated unless some degree of control over the situation has been achieved.

6. Time management skills

One of the basic tenets of crisis intervention as a method of helping people in difficulties is that intensive short-term work is far more effective than less intensive work over a longer period (see Chapter 4 below).

What this means, in effect, is that the crisis worker is expected to devote a large amount of time to each case, as this is cost effective in the long run. This being the case, time management becomes a very significant issue, especially for those people who work in settings where newly referred crisis situations must compete for priority with existing long-term non-crisis work.

Developing an effective and flexible time management system and the skills required to operate it optimally is therefore a key part of the crisis worker's repertoire. Having such a flexible system is, after all, a coping mechanism and, as such, it helps us to maintain homeostasis and thus reduce the risk of a personal crisis on our part.

To carry out a good assessment of a crisis situation involves being in the right place at the right time, and so considerable flexibility is needed. However, those who opt for total flexibility, at the expense of a system, run the risk of losing control of their workload and losing track of priorities. The fact that someone is in crisis does not automatically mean that he or she is a priority compared with other work tasks. The priorities need to be assessed in the context of the knowledge that crisis theory gives us of the helping potential of crisis, but this should not blind us to the need to appreciate competing priorities. For example, rushing out to deal with a minor crisis may mean we are not available when a much more serious crisis arises. Technology can be of assistance here in terms of mobile phones and so on, but these cannot be a substitute for a system of managing our time to maximum effect.

Acquiring time management skills is by no means an easy task, but the efforts required should be repaid, with dividends, by the rewards of such a set of useful skills.

7. Holistic thinking

This refers to the ability to get an overview of a situation. In an earlier work (Thompson, 2006b) I referred to it as 'helicopter vision', the ability to rise above a situation and get the 'big picture'. This is an important principle for practice in general, but is particularly important in crisis situations, as the pressures, demands and timescales of a crisis situation can easily lead to people (including professional helpers) losing sight of the wider context of what is happening.

Holistic thinking is a significant aspect of high-quality assessment because, without it, we can:

- Be seduced into crisis survival, aiming for a return to the pre-crisis state, rather than aiming to capitalise on the positive potential of the situation
- Neglect important aspects of the social context, such as gender dynamics, racism and so on.
- Allow the tensions of the situation to distract us from the calm, level-headed approach that is needed.

It is therefore essential that we develop the skills of holistic thinking, of looking beyond the immediate presenting problems and the direct pressures on us at the time.

8. Self-care skills

This is probably the most important set of skills of all. Crisis work can be very pressurised, demanding, challenging and potentially harmful to one's health and well-being. Many workers find crisis intervention exciting, exhilarating and very rewarding, but this can very easily turn sour in a number of ways. This is again particularly the case in the very demanding assessment stage where no clear plan of work has emerged, where feelings are running high and where the people involved are unknown to us. In view of this potential danger, there is a clear need for a strong emphasis on self-care. This is important for two reasons: first, for the obvious personal benefit of the helper and, second, for the benefit of clients; a crisis worker on sick leave due to nervous exhaustion is not much use to his or her clients. Cutting corners on self-care is therefore a false economy.

In Chapter 6, I shall address issues of staff care and workplace well-being, the responsibilities I feel employers have for safeguarding and supporting their staff. What I wish to emphasise here, however, is *self*-care, the part played by employees rather than employers. The two sets of issues, self-care and staff care, should of course interlock, but the absence of one should not be allowed to hinder the development of the other. Both elements are important, if not crucial.

Skill development can be directed towards the following areas:

- *Time out* Despite the demands of crisis, time must be found for 'time out'. This should be in the form of regular breaks, extra hours worked being taken as 'time off in lieu', time to think, relax, and discuss (such 'reflective practice' should be part of the time-management system referred to above). A worker who gets caught up in the hectic pace of a crisis needs to slow the pace as far as possible and actually manage the situation – and this should include allowing space for time out. Crisis workers who contribute to their own pre-mature burnout are not doing their clients, their employers, themselves or their profession any favours.

- *Protection* Crisis situations are often potential sources of violence; in many cases the worker may become involved either coincidentally, by being in the wrong place at the wrong time, or as a direct result of his or her role – for example, the compulsory hospitalisation of a mentally disordered person or the removal of a child to a place of safety. Where such potential violence is anticipated, the worker should insist on having a colleague present, or even a police officer, if the risk is significantly high. Other conflict management techniques for preventing or avoiding violence can also be drawn upon (see Chapter 6). Developing the appropriate skills is therefore very much to be encouraged.

- *Drawing the line* When crisis work gets the adrenaline flowing, it may become difficult to 'switch off' and draw the line between work and home life. There is a little point having the discipline to take much needed breaks during work time if one's personal and social life is dominated by work issues or anxieties. 'Drawing the line' is therefore vital, as trying to cope with other people's crises 24 hours a day is a certain recipe for disaster – the perennial danger: crisis work produces a crisis in the worker. Methods of relaxing and switching off from work should therefore be actively sought.

This is of course not an exhaustive list, but it is to be hoped that it will suffice to emphasise the point that neglecting the development of self-care skills is a risky business, and is not only potentially disastrous, but also positively courts disaster.

The eight skill areas outlined here are basic building blocks of good assessment work and, as we have emphasised, good assessment is particularly important in crisis work, as the timescale of the whole operation is so telescoped.

Most, if not all, of these skills will be needed for, and relevant to, the intervention stage proper, as assessment and intervention tend to merge anyway. The distinction between the two stages is, of course, more a matter of emphasis than a hard and fast boundary. But, before moving on to consider strategies of intervention, let us first round off our examination of assessment by outlining some common pitfalls which require careful navigation if they are to be avoided.

Pitfalls to be avoided

The full range of potential pitfalls across the full panoply of crisis situations is, of course, a very broad one indeed. For present purposes, then, I will focus on five potential pitfalls in particular.

1. Crisis begets crisis

This is perhaps something of a leitmotif in this work, but I feel it is sufficiently important to merit such emphasis. It is in fact two pitfalls in one. On the one hand, it means that the worker's own coping resources need to be strong and extensive to prevent the situation also being a trigger for a crisis in the worker (in so far as existing coping mechanisms break down and homeostasis is destroyed). On the other hand, it means that where a crisis does occur on the worker's part, this needs to be recognised and dealt with accordingly. What we have learned from crisis theory applies not only to clients in crisis but also to employees. The twofold pitfall to avoid therefore is:

a) plunging into crisis oneself; and

b) where this does occur, failing to recognise the fact and therefore not seeking the appropriate help (as we shall see in Chapter 6, crisis work should not be a solitary activity).

2. Moving not at the client's pace

In the heat of crisis, it is a mistake all too easily made to press on as fast as possible, given the time constraints crisis intervention imposes, but thereby move too fast for the client(s). In crisis situations time is of the essence, but this is no excuse for not moving at the client's pace. It may well be necessary to try gently to speed up the client's pace at times – for example, through encouragement – but it is none the less important to adhere to that pace.

   Crisis intervention is geared towards helping to empower people in crisis to draw on the positive potential and thereby increase their coping resources and capabilities. This cannot be done except at the client's pace.

3. Seeing a crisis that is not there

Some situations are characterised by high drama and intense emotional impact but are not, in fact, crises. A crisis is the breakdown of routine coping methods, a discontinuity in homeostasis. Such dramatic incidents – for example, a heated argument in which violence is threatened – may be unusual, and suggestive of crisis to most people, but for some may be a routine way for coping and thus not a crisis at all. It would therefore be inappropriate to apply crisis intervention principles in such circumstances.

   It should be remembered that crisis is both a subjective and an objective phenomenon. No matter how dramatic or 'crisis-like' the objective circumstances may seem, if the subjective perceptions of the people involved do not lead to their seeing it as a crisis, it is not a crisis.

An inexperienced worker, dealing with a couple who yell at each other at the top of their voices, may not feel able to handle the situation but, if this is the case, his or her crisis as a worker should not be confused with a crisis on the couple's part.

The pitfall to be avoided, therefore, is that of seeing a crisis where none exists.

4. Failing to recognise the significance of conflict

A common feature of crisis is conflict, although this is something the 'pioneers' did not address. Indeed, conflict can be seen as a basic part of human interaction in general, and is therefore likely to feature all the more at times of crisis, given the additional pressures and tensions involved. Seeing conflict as a characteristic of human existence is a key part of existentialist philosophy, as discussed in Chapter 1. (See Sartre, 1976. This is particularly the case when that existence is characterised by such oppressive social divisions as class, race, gender and so on, which bring with them conflicts at various levels.)

If we accept that conflict is part and parcel of crisis, surely arriving at a resolution to the conflict is a short cut to dealing with the crisis? In reality, we must answer 'no' to this question. This is because it is a problematic position to adopt, partly because it is somewhat naive (is a conflict-free situation feasible or is it idealistic to expect this?) and partly because it would amount to 'crisis survival' (see Chapter 1), rather than crisis intervention.

Against this background we should recognise that the crisis intervention task should not simply be to attempt to resolve the immediate conflict (although this may be a key part of the overall strategy), but rather to empower those in crisis to manage conflict more effectively and successfully.

The pitfall here, therefore, is to pursue an unattainable goal of a conflict-free situation, a consensus. Our aim, rather, should be one of gaining the strength and skills to handle conflict as and when it arises.

5. Seeking certainty

There are few certainties in life. However, in parallel fashion to pitfall number 4 above, we may often be seeking an unattainable goal of certainty when some semblance of probability may be the most that can be afforded.

The casework tradition of assessment prevalent in the early days of crisis intervention was based on a 'diagnosis' phase which entailed planning on the basis of as much relevant information as possible. As we have already seen, this approach is not appropriate to crisis intervention due to the urgency involved.

However, the strength of the traditional approach is that the degree of certainty/probability, upon which one bases one's intervention, is maximised. Crisis workers have to operate on much lower margins of probability. Seeking certainty, or even a high degree of probability before one acts is likely to amount to paralysis. The pace of crisis dictates a much less cautious approach (although this is no excuse for throwing all caution to the wind), otherwise there may be a hiatus between the assessment and intervention phases, and this is likely to result in 'missing the boat' as new and perhaps inappropriate coping mechanisms are adopted while the worker is still making up their mind about what to do.

This pitfall, therefore, is allowing one's intolerance of uncertainty to produce inaction or delay necessary action.

These, then, are just a few of the many pitfalls to be encountered in the minefield of crisis intervention in general and the assessment stage in particular. In combination with an understanding of the principles of crisis intervention and the associated skills, an awareness of these pitfalls will, it is to be hoped, help to equip workers to undertake good quality assessment of crisis situations and thus build a clear plan of intervention.

Conclusion

This chapter has emphasised the importance of assessment and, in doing so, has focused on principles, skills and pitfalls. My hope is that the discussions here will provide a platform for further learning and for the beginnings of practice in this important area.

Principles	Skills	Pitfalls
1. Early assessment is crucial	1. Listening skills	1. Crisis begets crisis
2. Both the subjective and the objective dimensions must be included	2. Reflecting feelings	2. Moving not at the client's pace
3. Reinforcing coping skills	3. Seeing a crisis that is not there	3. Assessment should not have a narrow, psychological focus
4. Information gathering	4. Focus on the positive	4. Failing to recognise the significance of conflict
5. Medicalisation should be avoided	5. Calming and being calm	5. Seeking certainty
6. Identifying the problem focus	6. Time-management skills	

7. Clear plans need to
   be formulated

7. Holistic thinking

8. A balanced approach to risk
   assessment is needed

8. Self-care skills

Figure 4:
Assessment

Having set the scene for a discussion of the actual process of intervention, let us now bring our analysis of assessment issues to a close and thereby move on to explore the how, where, when, what and why of crisis intervention.

Points to ponder

> ➤ What dangers might arise if a narrow, psychological approach to assessment is adopted rather than a broader psychosocial one?
> ➤ Why is it important to reinforce coping skills?
> ➤ Why is it important to work at the client's pace?

Chapter 4
Intervention

Introduction

Crisis theory may well be a valuable guide to understanding what happens in crises and the way in which a crisis affects people. But how, you may be asking, can this be used in a pragmatic way to guide members of the helping professions in dealing with people in crisis? Chapter 3 has shown us how the insights can be used to assess the situation, but this is a long way from actually doing something about resolving the situation. So, to put it technically: how can crisis theory be operationalised, how can it 'pay its dues' by being of clear, positive and direct help to crisis workers?

In order to try to answer these questions, this chapter will follow the same basic pattern as Chapter 3. I shall first of all spell out what I see as the basic principles of crisis intervention, followed by a discussion of the skills workers need to develop in order to use these principles as an effective guide to practice. Finally, I shall examine some of the pitfalls to be avoided, some of the mistakes that can easily be made in the fraught atmosphere of crisis.

It needs to be recognised that, although I am aiming to bridge theory and practice, I cannot provide a simple formula for workers to follow. I can, however, provide a framework which is not simply 'interesting', but can also be of practical value in helping people cope positively with crises.

I shall begin with what I see as the eight principles which govern crisis intervention.

Principles of crisis intervention

These principles are based on a wide range of sources, including my own practice experience, but in particular I should acknowledge reference to the classic work of Ewing (1978) and Morrice (1976).

1. Delay in intervention tends to be costly

The sooner intervention begins, the better. During the impact and recoil stages of crisis, there is little that can be done by way of positive steps forward, as the participants tend to be emotionally numbed and thus unresponsive. However, being involved in the early stages has three advantages, as follows:

a) Early assessment can begin.

b) Simply 'being there' helps to engage the client(s) and thereby set the scene for positive intervention. This can make a very significant difference in terms of forming a positive working relationship, as such presence will generally be very much appreciated, both at the time and later.

c) Appropriate resources (support networks and so on) can be mobilised or identified ready for mobilisation at the appropriate time.

When a crisis situation is encountered, considerable nervous energy is generated, and this sudden thrust of energy can be a source of strong motivation and determination. This is a major resource which both clients and professional workers can draw upon as part of the problem-solving process. Previous routine patterns of behaviour are likely to be abandoned and new ways of coping can be sought. This is a very fruitful time for intervention to take place, as the nervous energy characteristic of crisis can be harnessed positively and used constructively to try to make whatever changes are necessary to resolve the crisis and capitalise upon it.

At such a highly charged, volatile and threatening time, it is very tempting indeed to use 'crisis survival' techniques – for example, by waiting for things to 'cool down' by staying off the scene for a while. The net result of such a strategy is likely to be to 'miss the boat' by failing to make the most of the change resources produced by the crisis.

If intervention is delayed, the client(s) may have resolved the crisis in some other way and may thus produce a solution which is not going to be helpful when future stresses and potential crises are brewing. For example, a woman who becomes disabled may give up her job because, still in crisis, she cannot cope with the pressures. The loss of job, income, status, social contacts and so on thus makes her more vulnerable to crisis. The short-term gain (crisis survival) is a longer-term loss. Early intervention could perhaps have helped her cope with the job in the interim, or arrange 'time out', thus seeking a more positive outcome of the crisis.

The fact that crisis intervention requires early involvement has serious implications for the organisational structure in which the crisis worker operates; a system which takes two weeks or more to allocate or respond to referrals more or less kills the opportunity for optimal crisis intervention. This is a point to which I shall return in Chapter 6.

2. Intensive short-term work is more effective than extensive long-term work

This is related to the first principle, namely the value of early intervention. Putting in a great deal of effort to produce constructive change pays dividends in the long run, as the crisis produces the energy and motivation to develop stronger and more effective methods of coping which will:

a) help to prevent future crises;

b) improve confidence and self-esteem, and

c) contribute to a better quality of life.

Because clients tend to be more receptive to help when they are in crisis, considerable movement towards desired goals can be achieved in a relatively short period of time, carried by the vehicle of the motivation generated by the crisis. The 'fight or flight' mechanism, if channelled positively, can direct the client's actions towards effective problem solving and thus build up coping resources.

These resources are, as I stressed earlier, not simply psychological ones, but also include wider familial, community, social and institutional ones. The response of significant individuals, groups or agencies will often be stronger and more supportive in times of crisis than at times of routine requests for assistance. The energy and drama of the crisis can therefore 'suck in' external coping resources in ways which do not apply to non-crisis situations. For example, housing departments or associations may well be more sympathetic to a family's housing problems when a crisis situation obtains than is usually the case.

In long-term work much time, effort and energy are expended in seeking to motivate clients towards constructive change. This is so often an uphill struggle; clients quite understandably tend to offer much resistance, as the situation implies an externally defined change – that is, change on the professional helper's terms rather than the client's. This is very problematic, as this comment from Marris illustrates:

> To be told the meaning of your life by others, in terms which are not yours, implies that your existence does not matter to them, except as it is reflected in their own. (1986, p. 155)

This is a major 'occupational hazard' for long-term workers who may be geared more towards 'maintaining' a situation – that is, the focus is on preventing deterioration, rather than bringing about improvement (Thompson, 2009c). Crisis workers are in a much more 'luxurious' position in terms of the positive potential for change. Realising that potential can thus obviate the need for later long-term work.

3. Listening is a key activity

Crisis workers are in a powerful position in dealing with clients who are vulnerable and relatively helpless at that time. It is therefore extremely important that the trouble is taken actually to listen to what clients are saying. As I shall stress below, providing the 'right answer' without listening to clients is of no help and potentially very harmful. Intervention needs to take account of both the objective and subjective dimensions for, as we have seen, crisis operates at, and affects, both of these aspects. The latter dimension, that of the subjective area of perceptions, emotions and values, necessarily involves listening. To operate purely or mainly at the objective level – where the professional helper is relatively powerful - amounts merely to crisis survival, as it does not equip the client(s) to cope any better with the next crisis. The subjective dimension can be an intense area with potent emotional storms and a devastating sense of loss. Here, the helper feels powerless and can easily feel overwhelmed by the raw emotion. Because of this, listening can be painful, distressing and can itself provoke a crisis in the helper. Good practice in crisis intervention must none the less be premised on good and effective listening (and 'listening' can also be understood to refer, metaphorically, to being sensitive to nonverbal communication).

Listening is, of course, a key aspect of assessment and therefore plays an important part in the early stages, but the point I am making here is that it is vital to keep listening throughout the intervention process. In crisis, both feelings and circumstances can change rapidly, and so the crisis worker needs to remain 'tuned in' to the crisis scenario.

4. A repertoire of methods is available

Crisis intervention is not a specific method which implies the exclusion of other methods. Rather, it is a theoretical framework which guides us in certain directions and provides certain insights, but which does not offer a simple formula for 'putting things right'.

One of the basic tenets of crisis theory is that human existence is complex, fraught, vulnerable and uncertain, hence the need for us to equip ourselves, both socially and psychologically, for the pressures, trauma and crises implicit in such an existence. Given this model, a step-by-step prescription for practice would be both inadequate and inappropriate.

The framework of crisis intervention assumes that there is a wide repertoire of coping skills and resources which can be drawn upon in our efforts to help. In parallel fashion, a repertoire of helping methods (as discussed in Chapter 2) can be drawn upon to fulfil the goals identified by making use of a crisis intervention framework.

At a theoretical/conceptual level, crisis intervention may be contradicted by other approaches. For example, crisis theory is premised on human freedom and responsibility for one's actions, while the behaviourist psychology on which cognitive behavioural work is premised eschews such notions as idealistic. However, at the level of practice, useful and effective behavioural techniques can be uprooted from their deterministic background and 'replanted' in the more humanistic context of crisis theory. This amounts not to using behaviourism instead of crisis intervention, but rather to using behavioural methods (for example, the reinforcement of positives) in a way which is consistent with, and therefore part of, a crisis intervention programme.

The theoretical issues relating to the problem of using fundamentally incompatible approaches need not concern us here (see Thompson, 2010, for a discussion of these issues in relation to social work but which also has implications for other branches of the helping professions). Suffice to note that crisis intervention does not compete with other approaches or methods, but rather provides an overarching framework which helps to guide, and illuminate, our practice.

Behavioural psychology has been chosen as an example, but the same argument applies to family therapy, Rogerian counselling, transactional analysis or whatever other tool we choose to employ.

5. Intervention should be future oriented

Crisis involves a significant element of loss and especially loss of control; it is therefore not surprising that clients should concentrate on the past, either as part of a grieving process or as part of an attempt to make sense of what has led to the present confused and painful situation. This in itself is helpful, but it can easily take up excessive time and energy and prevent the client from moving on.

Where this situation becomes problematic, it is often described as 'crying over spilled milk'. A fundamental premise of crisis intervention is that the focus should be on future planning, not on past mistakes.

A crisis generates considerable nervous energy and motivation and this needs to be focused on future actions, on how to cope better in respect of the next crisis and the one after that, and so on. Working out what mistakes were made previously may form a part of this, but it should be limited to a small part, as once again the emphasis should be on positive strengths, as building self-confidence is a crucial part of developing new coping skills or exploring/cultivating new support systems.

Focusing on the future is also very significant in terms of generating hope – again a key element in crisis intervention – as hope is a reflection of our (positive) attitude to the future.

A crisis is a situation which has overpowered us, which appears to have minimised our control over our circumstances, over our lives. In these conditions we are literally 'alienated' – we feel that our lives are not our own. Reinstating this sense of ownership of our own lives is a fundamental part of instilling hope and bringing about post-crisis rebuilding.

Part of this future orientation is the need to avoid attributing blame. Whether this blame is directed inwards towards oneself as guilt or outwards towards others as censure, it has little or no therapeutic value and should therefore be discouraged.

To pinpoint who is or was to blame may possibly clarify who or what contributed to the crisis or it may cloud the issue. Regardless of this, from a therapeutic point of view, attributing blame is unhelpful, as it prevents the client(s) from moving on.

Crisis workers should therefore discourage this and should most certainly avoid engaging in it themselves, although clients in crisis will often pressurise workers to do so in order to reinforce their own view of who is to blame.

6. Intervention should be time limited

One of the key characteristics of crisis as identified by the classical theory of crisis intervention is that of being 'time limited'. Crises are relatively short lived; we tend to 're-equilibrate' ourselves fairly quickly, as homeostasis is far preferable to the worry and anguish of crisis. Intervention should also reflect this by having a clear, but flexible time limit.

One of the dangers of working with people in crisis is that they can become dependent on us. The crisis worker can be viewed as a coping resource to be drawn upon when future crises loom, and this can demotivate clients from developing their own coping skills or 'plugging in' to appropriate support systems. It is therefore important that the crisis worker does not stay involved any longer than is necessary and makes it clear that his or her involvement will be only temporary.

A useful strategy for achieving this is to state explicitly in the early stages of intervention that help will be offered only while needed – that is, on a short-term basis. This can be the basis of a contract, an agreed set of shared objectives to be pursued within a realistic timescale (realistic in terms of the predicted timescale of the crisis).

There are two major advantages to this strategy:

i) It does not give false expectations about a prolonged period of intervention and support.

ii) It introduces a degree of control and stability into a situation characterised by absence of control and equilibrium.

Time-limited contract work is therefore a popular option for those workers who favour a crisis intervention approach. There are, however, two 'riders' which need to be added to this in order to avoid the potential drawbacks of this strategy. These are:

i) Time targets must be flexible. It is pointless closing a case or otherwise terminating our helping role simply because the agreed timescale has expired. The matter should be brought to a close only when the agreed initial (or renegotiated) objectives have been met or accepted as unattainable. The discipline of a timescale should therefore be seen as a means to an end, rather than an end in itself.

ii) When our intervention is brought to a close, clients are likely to need the reassurance that they are not debarred from future help if or when this is required. In other words, it needs to be made clear that bringing our intervention to an end does not amount to 'closing the door' for good. Very often the security offered by knowing that a 'safety net' exists can give people the confidence to cope (I shall re-emphasise this again below).

Time-limited intervention should therefore not be used as an inappropriate tool of workload management by closing cases prematurely.

7. Crisis intervention is proactive

One of the common misunderstandings of crisis intervention is that it is reactive – that is, that it is not preventative. Of course, this is most certainly not the case; the primary aims of crisis intervention are to facilitate the learning of new and better coping skills and greater use of support networks. These activities are clearly proactive in so far as they are geared towards preventing future crises.

However, what should also not be forgotten is that this does not limit us to waiting for crises to happen (or worse still, playing the potentially disastrous game of deliberately provoking crises), as the principles of crisis intervention can equally be applied on a much wider basis. For example, members of the helping professions can become involved in training people in coping skills, especially when it comes to those people who may be more prone to crisis (such as people with mental health problems). Similarly, other forms of preventative work – for example, benefit take-up campaigns to help alleviate poverty – are consistent with crisis intervention.

In terms of prevention, crisis intervention gives us two messages:

i) Any work which helps to prevent crises is to be encouraged. This includes reducing stress/distress on the one hand and boosting coping skills and support networks on the other.

ii) Effective crisis intervention should teach people how to prevent future crises where possible and how to cope better with those that cannot be prevented.

8. A psychosocial approach is needed

The point has already been emphasised that traditional approaches to crisis intervention tended to adopt a narrow, individualistic perspective that paid little or no attention to the wider social context, even though social factors, both cultural and structural, can be seen to be major factors in crisis situations. It is therefore important to adopt a psychosocial approach – that is, one which incorporates an understanding of not only psychological factors, but also sociological ones. Without this broader approach there is a danger that we will miss key issues, especially those that relate to discrimination and oppression.

These, then, are the major principles of crisis intervention, but of course many other such principles could be deduced if time and space permitted. Having outlined these practice principles, we now need to make them more concrete and more accessible by discussing the skills that I see as being necessary for putting such principles into practice – that is, for converting crisis theory into crisis intervention. I shall follow the same pattern as for the previous chapter by outlining the relevant skills before moving on to discuss pitfalls to be avoided.

Crisis intervention skills

What needs to be made clear from the outset is that the skills already discussed in relation to crisis assessment will also be very relevant and valuable in the intervention phase proper. In particular, the ability to listen, to reflect feelings and to reinforce coping skills are key parts of effective intervention.

1. Risk management

The importance of risk assessment was emphasised in Chapter 3. However, situations change over time, often very quickly in a crisis scenario, and so the risk configuration can also change quickly. So, while the initial risk assessment may have been highly accurate, it may be inappropriate not long after. This means that risk management means having a clear picture of the risk factors and how they are changing, rather than relying on a relatively static initial risk assessment.

Crisis workers therefore need to develop the skills of risk management – that is, the ability to be tuned in to the risk issues involved in a situation and to retain a balance. This balance involves avoiding the extremes of complacency (the reckless disregard of significant hazards) on the one hand and paranoia on the other (adopting too rigid and cautious an approach to risk that can be counter-productive and even oppressive). This is not an easy balance to maintain, and no doubt we will get it wrong from time to time, but if we settle for either of the destructive extremes, it is likely that we will get it wrong much of the time.

2. Patience

Patience may be a virtue, but it is also a skill. It is related to the concept, introduced earlier, of working at the client's pace.

Crisis work can be very frustrating and can seriously try our patience. It is something of an 'occupational hazard' to have to resist strong feelings of moving the client quickly on when he or she is not yet ready to make progress. Conversely, a client may wish to hurtle on at breakneck speed, while the worker feels a gentler pace is more prudent.

The worker's patience may be tested in a number of other ways:

- important advice may be ignored or notes of caution may go unheeded;
- a key member of the support network may withdraw;
- co-operation from other professionals may be lacking or they may adopt a judgmental or oppressive standpoint (for example, racist, sexist or ageist); and/or
- the institutional resources needed may not be available.

The danger here is to fall into the essentialist trap of seeing patience as a quality which some people have but which others do not. Patience is a skill or a pattern of behaviour which can be learned or developed. As crisis intervention tends to make demands on one's patience, it pays dividends to develop this skill, or set of skills - controlled emotional expression, unconditional positive regard, the ability to think clearly and work effectively while under pressure. These all come under the umbrella of patience and are indispensable components of the crisis worker's repertoire. They are not inbred parts of one's personality, but rather skills and behaviour which can be learned and improved through practice, effort and discussion.

3. Confrontation

Diplomacy is clearly recognised as an important skill in the helping professions in general, and is of no less value in crisis intervention in particular. Tactlessness is certainly no advantage in crisis work. However, there are times when diplomacy needs to be counterbalanced by the appropriate and skilful use of confrontation.

As clients enter the exit phase of the crisis, they may adopt unhelpful, counterproductive or harmful methods of coping, such as excessive drinking or other forms of avoidance behaviour. In such circumstances, it will be the task of the crisis worker to effect a confrontation, but without alienating the clients concerned. This involves a delicate and subtle balance, and thus a skilled approach is called for.

This is parallel with the notion of 'non-provocative probing' applied in the earlier assessment phase – the need to tackle delicate issues firmly but sensitively. As noted in Chapter 3, crises are characterised by conflicts of various kinds, and so effective crisis intervention entails being able and willing to confront such conflicts head on (albeit tactfully, skilfully and constructively), thus helping clients to move on by resolving, or learning how to manage, the conflicts they encounter.

Skilful confrontation hinges on a number of factors:

• the courage to tackle painful, anxiety-provoking or contentious issues;
• the ability to work calmly under such pressures (and also to instil calmness);
• self-awareness in recognising and dealing with one's own feelings and interests in relation to the conflictual situation;
• good communication. Care should be taken to ensure that confrontation is not interpreted as a personal attack or aggression.

Thus, there are two extremes to steer clear of: avoiding confrontation on the one hand (the 'safety first' approach); and using it overzealously on the other (the 'over-the-top' approach). It is a matter of having the skills to confront key issues without being confrontational.

4. Motivation and self-motivation

Like patience, self-motivation is something which is seen in commonsense terms as a quality rather than a skill. However, crisis theory is an example of an approach which denies 'essentialism', the view that we are burdened or otherwise with fixed characteristics. Our patterns of behaviour and thought reflect our characteristic methods of coping and our skills, rather than a fixed essence. Consequently, we can learn to motivate ourselves; we can learn to seek satisfaction from the work we do. It is to be hoped that reading texts such as this can be part of that process.

Crises produce considerable nervous energy and, as Chapter 2 illustrated, this can be used either positively or negatively. The energy is produced not only in the clients and their associates, but also potentially in the worker. Positive use of crisis entails using this energy to motivate ourselves.

Crises are a minefield of several different emotions for all concerned. In carrying out crisis intervention, the professional helper can be prone to frustration, fear, anger, even depression and must be able not only to cope with these, but also to instil positive feelings in clients and in him- or herself – that is, to motivate and be motivated. There are a range of skills involved in this: primarily communication skills on the one hand (motivation), and self-awareness skills on the other (self-motivation). It is therefore an unacceptably easy way out to say 'self-motivation is not one of my strong points'. Being involved in crises means that our thoughts, feelings and patterns of behaviour are often 'on the line', and we are vulnerable to criticism and self-criticism. Crisis work is not a 'safe', comfortable or clinical approach to helping people; this means that opportunities to learn about ourselves and build on what we learn are never very far away.

The need to build upon such learning is also ever-present. This is an exciting and challenging aspect of crisis work and is a key element in the art of self-motivation. Being self-motivated in itself goes some way towards motivating others, as it sets a positive tone for the intervention. This can be supplemented by 'motivational interviewing' techniques (Miller and Rollnick, 2002) and also by advocacy or other forms of helping to change the objective circumstances which may be demotivating. This is consistent with the principle that both the subjective and the objective dimensions of the situation must be taken into account.

5. Ending

I have already argued that intervention should be time limited in order to prevent dependency. One of the major implications of this is that professional helpers, as we build up experience of crisis work, should seek to develop the skills of ending intervention as effectively as possible.

It is not enough simply to announce that involvement is to cease. It is to be hoped that, by this stage the client(s) will be much stronger and thus less vulnerable. None the less, a badly handled termination may undo much of the good which has previously been done. At this stage in the proceedings, a client's confidence is likely to be rather tentative and somewhat precarious. It is therefore unwise to risk this by withdrawing abruptly. This may provoke a further crisis.

One of the characteristics of crisis we have identified is the lack of control, the breakdown of homeostasis. Part of the crisis worker's task is to help bring the situation under control. The client may therefore come to associate control and stability with the worker and thus feel very threatened by his or her withdrawal from the scene. Ending intervention therefore needs to be handled carefully and sensitively.

As with any other situation which needs to be managed carefully, there are three clear dimensions to this:

- *Analysis* The component parts of the situation need to be recognised and understood.
- *Planning* A haphazard, 'take it as it comes' approach is unnecessarily risky. The ending phase is not just the close of intervention, but rather a key part of that intervention. Planning therefore has an important role to play.
- *Control* The crisis worker needs to take some degree of responsibility for the situation and ensure that it goes to plan, as far as is practicable.

This model is also applicable to the types of intervention where ending involvement is likely to be welcomed by the clients involved. An example of this would be a child protection case that has been resolved. Although the situation may be such that the case can safely be closed, the feelings generated by the crisis may lead to bitterness and considerable ill-feeling or even emotional harm if the ending of intervention is rushed or mishandled.

6. Integrating theory and practice

Professional training courses have long stressed the value and importance of relating theory to practice. This is often a cause for concern among students as there is no clear, straightforward way of translating theory into practice, and yet the need to do so is constantly emphasised. This is an important principle of reflective practice, the idea that professional practice is not simply 'painting by numbers' – it requires certain skills in terms of being able to translate the professional knowledge base into a useful foundation for practice (Thompson and Thompson, 2008a).

The same situation obtains in relation to crisis intervention. Crises are fraught, complex and demanding; it is therefore not possible simply to apply a formula or standardised approach. However, there still remains considerable value in drawing upon a professional knowledge base for, as we have warned, dealing with crises in a 'commonsense' way amounts to 'crisis survival', an ineffective and potentially harmful response to crisis. In short, doing 'crisis intervention' without reference to crisis theory is, in effect, not crisis intervention, but rather this poor relation called 'crisis surival'.

There is a set of skills involved in integrating theory and practice. Many practitioners avoid developing these skills by adopting the anti-intellectual stance of claiming to prefer to 'stick to practice'. For those who take a less ostrich-like approach to the rather thorny issues of integrating theory and practice, the appropriate skills need to be developed. As a first step towards this, we can readily identify some of the skills which are particularly appropriate in drawing on crisis theory in action:

• recognising the 'stages' (impact/recoil/exit);
• identifying positives to build on;
• encompassing the subjective and objective dimensions;
• recognising both the psychological and the wider social aspects.

These are, of course, only a small selection from a wide range, but it is to be hoped that this will at least give a flavour of practice grounded in theory.

7. Anti-discriminatory practice

For some time now the helping professions have been committed to paying serious attention to issues of oppression and discrimination on the grounds of class, race, gender, age, disability and sexual orientation and related matters (Thompson, 2006a). In many areas, explicit equal opportunities or diversity policies exist, at a rhetorical level at least, and the helping professions have made strenuous efforts to take these issues on board.

There has therefore been progress at a policy level (although there is a long way to go yet), but to date little attention has been paid to the actual skills required to practise in an anti-discriminatory way.

There is a strong parallel here with the question of integrating theory and practice.A body of knowledge is being developed (anti-discriminatory policy/ theory/ values), but there is then a quantum leap to the grassroots level of practice, with often only a very vague and sketchy bridge between the two.

Addressing these issues satisfactorily is far beyond the scope of this text but, on a more realistic scale, we can consider some of the skills issues which arise in relation to anti-discriminatory crisis work.

One of the key skills must be developing a sensitivity to the impact of social divisions on clients' lives. For example, in a family crisis, gender roles and patriarchal social relations are likely to feature significantly. If, for example, that family were black, the oppression of racism would also merit being taken into account.

The other side of this is, of course, our own potential for discrimination. In keeping with crisis theory, we need to consider both the objective dimension (the effects of discrimination on clients in terms of social pressures, coping skills and support networks), and the subjective (our own attitudes, values, assumptions which are brought to bear in our work). Anti-discriminatory practice entails recognising the impact of oppression on clients and how discriminatory ideologies (racism, sexism, ageism and so on) impinge upon and subtly influence our thoughts, feelings, attitudes and actions. After years of relative neglect, the helping professions are now addressing both sets of issues. Crisis intervention can be no exception to this. In the heat of crisis, professional helpers are pressurised yet powerful people, and so the potential for oppression and discrimination being unintentionally reproduced or reinforced presents a scenario which requires skilful handling.

8. Managing conflict

The point was made earlier that conflict is part and parcel of everyday life and is especially prevalent at times of crisis, given the additional pressures and tensions involved. The most effective and successful crisis workers are therefore likely to be those who have developed conflict managements skills and a range of conflict management methods.

At the other extreme, someone who has little or no confidence in dealing with conflict and who prefers to shy away from it is likely to be ill prepared for dealing effectively with the challenges involved in crisis situations and capitalising on the positive potential.

Managing conflict can involve advanced-level skills, but much of it involves the effective use of basic people skills – listening especially. Perhaps the most important step to begin with is not to run away from conflict. This can be a very small but significant step.

Some of the skills outlined here are well established and much in evidence in good practice across various agencies and settings. For other skills, however, there are fewer role models, fewer guidelines and less clarity. The challenge for crisis workers is therefore not simply to learn traditional skills, but also to forge new skills in building a crisis intervention which befits contemporary practice and values.

Pitfalls to be avoided

Crisis intervention is clearly quite a significant undertaking. With it comes a set of pitfalls that can lead to situations going awry. The following is not a comprehensive list, but it should be sufficient to paint a picture of how careful we need to be in practising crisis intervention.

1. False assumptions

These can be made by either client or worker – or both. Things happen fast in crisis, and it is therefore not surprising that communication can be reduced and important factors overlooked. Thus it is a simple but costly mistake to jump to conclusions. The pressure to get things done and 'strike while the iron is hot' can lead to assumptions being made which, in less pressurised times, would have been checked out.

This applies equally to clients and practitioners. Professional helpers can base their intervention on false assumptions or misinformation and therefore be off target in terms of the plans carried out. For example, a worker may send an important letter to a client, notifying him or her of an important issue, but then assume, perhaps wrongly, that the letter was received. Similarly a client may express an intention to discuss the situation with another significant party and, in the heat of crisis, the worker may assume that this has happened when in reality it may not have.

In parallel fashion, clients may base their actions on incorrect information or false assumptions. It is to be hoped that this is something that will have been picked up at the assessment stage, but it can easily be missed and then emerge at a crucial point in the intervention process. For example, a child care crisis may arise as a result of marital conflict. This conflict may be founded on a misunderstanding (and we know how often conflicts are based on misunderstanding) – for example, the unfounded suspicion of infidelity. Tension over one issue – for example, an accusation of child abuse – can easily spill over into other areas. Suspicion, mistrust and jumping to conclusions can therefore easily fan the flames of crisis and jeopardise the crisis worker's good efforts.

Consequently, crisis workers would do well to:

a) ensure that the pressure of crisis does not lead to panic-based false assump tions or a failure to make necessary checks;
b) be sensitive to the possibility that crises are founded on, or aggravated by, misinformation, misunderstanding or false assumptions.

2. Pathologising

One of the criticisms of traditional crisis theory introduced in Chapter 1 was the need to widen the focus on individual coping skills to include an understanding of the part played by wider social forces. This wider focus prevents us from seeing simply an individual 'pathology', a person who has failed or is inadequate. It helps to avoid falling into the trap of 'blaming the victim' (Ryan, 1988).

When a crisis occurs, it is the culmination of a range of psychological and social circumstances and forces putting excessive pressure on a person's (or a number of persons') homeostasis. To concentrate on one dimension only (the individual) and blame the crisis on his or her failings, foibles or fecklessness, is to oversimplify a complex psychosocial situation.

This process of blaming the victim amounts to 'pathologising' that person or persons. The individuals concerned are responsible for their actions and thus contribute in some ways to the crisis matrix. However, we perceive a distorted picture if we see only the dimension of the coping behaviours of the individuals concerned. The wider picture is represented diagrammatically in Figure 5.

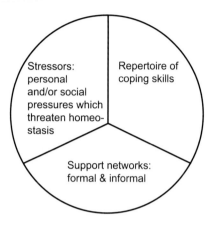

Figure 5: Dimensions of Stress

All three aspects, as illustrated in Figure 5. are important, as they are part of a complex interaction. We all have a coping repertoire, however limited or extensive this may be. Similarly, we all have some degree of support and we are all exposed to stressors of varying degrees. However, we should recognise the differential distribution of stressors and supports. For example, oppressed minorities face greater stressors – poverty, discrimination, hostility and so on – and yet may, at the same time, have fewer supports to draw upon – money, community organisations, accommodation and so on (see the discussion of 'social capital' in Castiglione et al., 2008). Thus the combination of the two may place excessive pressure on the third – the coping repertoire. However, we have to be wary of oversimplifying the situation and approaching it in a reductionist way. While there are general social patterns to be taken into consideration, there are also individual factors that need to be accounted for. For example, the coping skills of a person who frequently experiences crisis (and learns and grows from the experience) may be more advanced than another more privileged person, who is more sheltered from the stressors associated with social problems and has a powerful network of support.

Crisis workers therefore need to beware of pathologising clients by reducing the three elements to one, as this is unfair, unhelpful and discriminatory.

3. Creating dependency

One of the primary aims of crisis intervention is to maximise the positive potential of the crisis by facilitating the learning of new and better coping skills and the development of support networks. Thus, it is geared towards avoiding dependency and enhancing independence – it is a form of empowerment. Ironically, however, the net result can often be a degree of dependency as a result of the process of intervention going wrong in some way.

Dependency can arise in the following ways:

i) The helper may do too much *for* the client and not enough *with* him or her. Crises can be severely disabling, especially in the early stages, and doing things for clients is often a reality. However, they then need to be 'weaned off' this as soon as practicable.

ii) Clients can develop an emotional dependence on the worker by becoming overly fond of him or her. Going through a crisis together can at times form a close and strong emotional bond. Workers need to be wary of the dangers of too close a bond, as this could make bringing the intervention to a close extremely difficult, painful and counterproductive.

iii) If the helper uses a task-centred approach, the task may be achieved successfully when the client is motivated by the helper's involvement (extrinsic motivation). If the task does not become sufficiently motivating in itself (intrinsic motivation), the worker's withdrawal may result in the cessation of key tasks. Dependency therefore ensues.

These three examples of dependency – pragmatic, emotional and motivational – are serious dangers in crisis work and notable pitfalls to avoid.

4. Closing the door

Crisis intervention is a time-limited mode of helping. Therefore ending our involvement, which is a key part of any intervention, is particularly significant. A major pitfall here is that of 'closing the door'. This entails giving clients the impression that they have had their ration of the practitioner's time, effort and resources and no further help will be offered, even if very much needed. This can be very demoralising and can sap confidence. This situation can arise chiefly in two ways: either the worker can sow the seeds of doubt by withdrawing with undue haste, or there may be a misunderstanding on the client's part in which it is assumed that the practitioner deals only with crises.

I have already stressed the importance of ending intervention effectively. The pitfall of 'closing the door' is therefore a major obstacle to achieving this.

Helpful steps in overcoming this would be:

- gradual withdrawal (although not unduly prolonged), with an emphasis on reinforcing coping skills;
- ensuring support networks are in place and operational;
- above all, making it clear to the client(s) that the door remains open for further intervention, where appropriate, whether on a crisis or directly preventative basis.

5. Not seeing the wood for the trees

One of the common criticisms of individualistic approaches to helping is that they cannot 'rise above a series of cases' (Mills, 1970). In crisis work this is a particular danger, because the helper is geared towards determining and resolving the specific problematic areas which have provoked, or which are sustaining, this particular crisis for these particular clients. It is therefore understandable that there is a tendency to focus on what is specific to a single case rather than extrapolate the similarities and patterns across cases.

Intervention skills 6 and 7 above should go some way towards avoiding this pitfall. That is, integrating theory and practice helps to raise awareness of the underlying patterns of crisis and this limits the need to 'reinvent the wheel' for each case. Anti-discriminatory practice also draws attention to the shared patterns across cases, the commonalities of oppression and disadvantage amongst women, for example (Sunderland, 2004).

Good practice in crisis intervention entails both analysing the specifics and locating these within the broader framework of commonalities. A practice which fails to see the wood for the trees aligns itself with traditional crisis theory and all that this entails (see Chapter 1).

As indicated earlier, this is by no means an exhaustive list of pitfalls. It is to be hoped that it will raise levels of awareness of common dangers and potential errors and hence help to sensitise practitioners to the potential hazards of crisis intervention.

However, I would not wish to paint too negative a picture, as if crisis work were nothing but hazards. The emphasis in Chapter 2 was on the positive potential of crisis and this applies equally to the helper. There is considerable potential for very effective, successful and rewarding practice. It is my hope and intention that the practice guidelines I have presented here – principles, skills and pitfalls – will tilt the balance in a positive direction by facilitating the development of a theory-based, anti-discriminatory crisis intervention.

I shall now move on to look at some examples of such crisis intervention in action. So far, I have sought to update and expand crisis theory, to underscore the positive dimension of crisis and to explore the practice base of the assessment and intervention phases. Chapter 5 builds on these developments by presenting three case studies of crisis resolution. It is to these that we now turn.

Principles	Skills	Pitfalls
1. Delay in intervention tends to be costly	1. Risk analysis	1. False assumptions
2. Intensive short-term work is more effective than extensive long-term work	2. Patience	2. Pathologising
3. Listening is a key activity	3. Confrontation	3. Creating dependency
4. A repertoire of methods is available	4. Motivation and self-motivation	4. Closing the door
5. Intervention should be future oriented	5. Ending	5. Not seeing the wood for the trees
6. Intervention should be time limited	6. Integrating theory and practice	
7. Crisis intervention is proactive	7. Anti-discriminatory practice	
8. A psychosocial approach is needed	8. Managing conflict	

Figure 6: Intervention

Points to ponder

> ➢ Why is it important not to delay getting involved in a crisis situation?
> ➢ What do you understand by the idea of confronting issues without being confrontational?
> ➢ How can you make sure that your efforts to help do not result in dependency?

Chapter 5
Case Examples

Introduction

The aim in this chapter is to build on the principles, skills and theory base already highlighted, by exploring practical examples of crisis intervention in action.

The main content of the chapter comprises three case studies of practice carried out on the basis of an explicit crisis intervention approach. The three cases are actual examples of work undertaken. No elements have been changed, except for a few minor details and the names used, which are suitably disguised to maintain confidentiality. One of the cases derives from a child protection team, the second from a community mental health team, and the third from a specialist multidisciplinary drugs team.

The format for each case study is as follows:

i) Scenario
ii) Assessment
iii) Intervention
iv) Discussion

These case studies are intended as actual illustrations of crisis intervention. Their purpose is to 'bring the theory to life' by allowing links to be drawn between the theoretical concepts and the practice issues which emerge from the cases.

Case A

i) Scenario

The Davenport family were referred to the local child protection team by their health visitor, as a result of safeguarding concerns.

The family consisted of Mr and Mrs Davenport, aged 23 and 20 respectively and their 17 month-old baby, named Jane. The couple had married six months before Jane's birth and subsequently moved into rented accommodation. They had previously been living with Mr Davenport's parents.

The marriage was a hasty one precipitated by the pregnancy. The couple had known each other for only three months. Despite this, the health visitor had no concerns about the family until the paternal grandparents expressed their anxieties about bruises they had noticed on Jane. It was at this point that a referral was made to the child protection team.

ii) Assessment

In response to this referral, a member of the team visited the family and explained the concerns raised. Initially, Mr and Mrs Davenport suggested the bruising was caused by their pet dog 'jumping up' at Jane or by her self-inflicting the injuries with a rattle. However, they subsequently admitted they were responsible for the injuries and were prepared to accept ongoing help.

In accordance with the procedures for safeguarding children and young people, a case conference was held and the decision was made to place Jane's name on the child protection register. Work began with the family to assess the situation and plan intervention.

Soon after this, a further injury was detected by the paternal grandparents which, after medical examination, proved to be a hairline fracture of the child's femur. Again, the medical evidence did not match the parents' explanation. At this point it was felt necessary to apply for an emergency protection order in order to ensure Jane's safety. An order was granted and Jane was received into care and placed with foster carers.

In some ways, it could be argued that the intervention, by 'breaking up the family', had provoked a crisis. There was clearly a strong element of threat involved in the crisis, but there was also opportunity, not least to assess the circumstances surrounding the abuse and seek a constructive way forward.

The child protection worker's assessment highlighted a number of significant issues:

a) The family experienced a number of crises (including 'life crises') within a short period of time:

- pregnancy
- marriage
- childbirth
- setting up home independently
- the removal of their child from home.

b) Professional intervention was essential in order to begin a process of change to capitalise on the constructive energy generated by the reception into care crisis.

c) The emergency protection order had removed trust, but it was important for this to be built back up again.

d) Jane needed to remain in care until the reasons underlying the abuse could be understood and danger factors removed or controlled. It was necessary to act quickly in order to prevent the situation from 'drifting'.

A picture was painted of a family who were finding it difficult to cope with a number of new experiences, to the point where control was lost and Jane was injured. The impinging pressures included:

- lack of experience of independent living (including the financial pressures involved);
- a relationship which developed very quickly to marriage and parenthood without having the opportunity to mature;
- very high expectations on the part of the paternal grandparents.

It was important to give the parents space by listening and reflecting feelings, especially the anger they might feel about the situation. Overall, this allowed them to feel safe with the worker. It worked especially well when the worker was able to reframe the anger/frustration as fear and concern for their child.

As the trauma of the current crisis unfolded, the emphasis moved from immediacy to appropriate planning and intervention.

iii) Intervention

The aim of the parents throughout was to have their child returned. However, this had to happen within a framework of appropriate change/movement by the family and an acceptable degree of safety for the child. It was not simply a matter of returning to the status quo.

A short-term focused intervention was drawn up by the worker and Jane's parents. After some negotiation, a programme of six sessions was agreed. It was geared towards the following areas:

1. Jane's future;
2. the factors underlying the injuries;
3. the marital relationship and respective roles;
4. family pressures;
5. parenting skills; and
6. mutual interests and the development of the relationship.

During this period and beyond, it was agreed that one important feature was the need to maintain contact with Jane and the foster carers.

This was readily achieved and succeeded in developing a close relationship with the foster carers. This was advantageous to the process, as Mr and Mrs Davenport became more confident with Jane while in a protected learning environment. The energy produced by the crisis gave them a keenness to learn and to get to grips with their problems. Equally, this paid dividends in the sessions, as they were more relaxed and felt supported. This enabled them to deal with the negative dimension of the crisis – the anger, the loss and the sense of failure.

Each session produced different insights and issues which would begin to help communication between the couple.

In session 1, issues around a baby's needs were explored (for example, shelter, warmth, food, drink, stimulation), and who could and should provide these. This moved into how relationships develop and how important bonds are formed. The role of the father in this was emphasised so as to avoid the development of stereotypical gender roles which would thus place undue pressure on the mother in her role and potentially leave the father feeling left out. In addition, there was some movement away from a view of children as possessions, to the respect a child has a right to expect from his or her carers.

In session 2 the parents were able to discuss the injuries and how they occurred. A picture emerged of the practical and emotional problems they had encountered and it became clear that the financial pressures of setting up home, with a young child, on a low income had seriously exacerbated the situation.

Both parents felt uneasy with their relationship and their responsibility as parents. They were quite frightened and had become reliant on outside advice and guidance on how to cope. This produced a double bind: they felt they could not cope without social supports, and yet this felt like failure, as the grandparents gave them the message that 'we coped all right with you when you were Jane's age' – they were left feeling unskilled and inadequate.

It became clear that Jane was a child who produced some anxiety in her parents in that she had feeding problems (she was lactose intolerant), which in turn affected her health and her sleeping patterns. This tended to produce a vicious circle. This was the framework of events in which the injuries occurred.

However, the combination of support from family meetings, skills training from foster carers and supportive couples counselling allowed an atmosphere of honesty and openness. The parents experienced a process of empowerment and confidence building. Strands of these issues permeated all six sessions and allowed the parents to recognise the factors leading up to the injuries, and gave insights into how, as a couple, they could function best when communication channels are opened up.

During and following the sessions, the parents' contact with Jane increased to the point where weekend home leave was arranged. The foster carers took an active role in supporting Mr and Mrs Davenport and gave feedback on their progress throughout this period.

Ultimately, Jane was placed back home, initially with very close supervision, but this was scaled down some months later, as the parents were clearly coping very effectively. They had come out of the crisis stronger and better able to cope with their pressures and knowing where to get support if they needed it.

iv) Discussion

In this case there was not one single crisis, but a culmination of several. Each seems to have compounded the next until the situation necessitated outside influences in order to bring matters under control and produce positive change.

Early and intensive intervention and assessment were crucial in allowing the parents to use the situation constructively. In this way, the reception into care became a gateway to solutions rather than simply an additional problem.

It was important for the crisis worker to frame the intervention in such a way as to help the family appreciate the positive potential of the situation. The subjective dimension – the parents' perception of the events – was as important as the objective dimension.

The parents were able to enter the exit phase in a spirit of seeking empowerment. This would not have happened without the effective use of interpersonal skills – listening, reflecting, reinforcing coping skills and so on. Also, clear plans gave structure and boundaries to the clients and worker, and thus introduced an element of control into a situation in which control had been lost. The boundaries produced an arena in which it was felt safe to express emotions – anger, frustration, happiness and so on. But the focus was not simply on the psychological dimension of feelings; attention was also paid to the social dimension of support systems.

Short-term interventions in complex child protection cases can be anxiety provoking for workers. As in all crisis situations, it is important that the risk involved is carefully analysed. Obviously, in Jane's case this was an ongoing assessment – a recurrent process of 'hypothesis testing'.

However, it was a positive process which allowed movement and reinforced progress by providing constructive feedback and allowing supportive relationships to develop (for example, between parents and foster carers and between parents and grandparents).

The most important element of this case was the significant progress towards empowerment through new and effective coping methods and the development of a system of support.

A great deal of thought, time and effort went into this case and clearly not all cases would merit this amount of commitment. However, this heavy investment was justified by the very positive results achieved (and the severity of the case), thus illustrating one of the key principles of crisis intervention – that intensive short-term work is a 'stitch in time' that saves extensive long-term work and, potentially, a far worse crisis.

Case B

i) Scenario

Dawn Weston was referred to the community mental health team by her GP. The initial request was for a mental health assessment by an approved mental health professional. Both the GP and the consultant psychiatrist felt she needed to be admitted to hospital on a compulsory basis as she was suffering from severe post-natal depression.

Dawn was 26, as was her husband, Ron. Rachel was their first child. The family lived in a terraced house, which they were buying with the aid of a mortgage.

The pregnancy had been an unexceptional one and the actual birth, although two weeks premature, presented no complications. However, on returning home from hospital with Rachel, Dawn became suddenly and inexplicably depressed. She became withdrawn and uncommunicative. She insisted on staying close to Rachel but made no attempt to care for her or meet her needs in any way. It was Ron's concern about this that led to the GP's involvement which in turn led to a visit by the consultant psychiatrist. Both doctors felt hospitalisation was necessary and duly completed medical recommendation forms for admission under Section 2 of the Mental Health Act 1983.

ii) Assessment

After discussing the diagnosis and general situation with the two doctors, the approved mental health professional (AMHP) made a home visit.

An interview with Ron revealed that he was very concerned about Dawn but had no explanation for her sudden and drastic change of behaviour and mood. He was not aware of any difficulties or pressures which could have precipitated the change.

An interview with Dawn initially produced quite a negative response. She seemed to be assuming that the AMHP was there to receive Rachel into care. She therefore needed considerable reassurance concerning the status and purpose of the AMHP's visit.

Despite pressure from the GP and consultant to arrange urgent admission, the AMHP decided to make a further visit the following day.

This tactic paid dividends, as Dawn was much more responsive this time. Although depressed, she had realised, largely as a result of the AMHP's prompting, that she had reached the 'point of no return' – crisis point. She had realised, perhaps, that hospitalisation and separation from Rachel (the hospital had no child care facilities) were imminent, and therefore she was more receptive to help.

It soon became apparent that there was a serious problem in terms of the presence of Dawn's parents. When labour commenced, Dawn's parents had arrived to 'help out'. They installed themselves in the spare bedroom and set about organising the new baby's environment.

This appeared to have triggered off a re-emergence of problems previously experienced but never resolved. As a child, and especially a teenager, Dawn had felt dominated by her parents and, in particular, by their strict religious views. Dawn had responded to this by leaving home at the earliest opportunity (at 16). This caused her parents great pain and dismay and led to considerable conflict. For several years they were ashamed of their 'tearaway' daughter (as they saw her) and this made Dawn feel both guilty and relieved – guilty about the pain she had caused but relieved to be away from their oppression (as she saw it).

When, a few years later, Dawn became engaged and then married, relations with her parents improved significantly, especially as Dawn was able to keep them at arm's length and not let them take over.

However, just as Dawn was adjusting to the 'life crisis' of Rachel's arrival, unresolved feelings and issues in relation to her parents were brought rapidly to a head by their attempts to 'help' – that is, by taking over Dawn's household.

Dawn, in her weakened physical state, felt unable to cope with the combination of pressures and felt unsupported by her husband who, she felt, had colluded with her parents. This situation had produced a crisis, to which Dawn responded by becoming depressed – the energy generated by the crisis was turned inwards as depression.

iii) Intervention

Dawn felt as though she had lost control; once again her life was not her own. It was therefore necessary to help her regain control, to take charge. This was accomplished by the following steps:

1. Dawn's parents were persuaded to pack their bags and return home. It was put to them that Dawn needed more time to herself to sort her feelings out. They were initially reluctant to comply with this, but the authority inherent in

the AMHP role (that is, the power to sanction Dawn's compulsory admission to hospital) was perhaps enough to persuade them to accept the advice.
2. Ron arranged to take time off work to be with Dawn and to contribute fully to caring for Rachel. Dawn's earlier comments about Ron had suggested that, while he fully wished to be helpful and supportive, his traditional views about the family and gender roles had erected barriers. The crisis, however, appeared to have enabled Ron to break down some of these barriers and to take on caring tasks he had previously seen as not being within his domain.
3. The worker offered three sessions to Dawn and Ron with the aim of clarifying/resolving:

a) Dawn's feelings towards her parents;

b) Dawn's religious and moral views (it had emerged in discussion that Dawn rejected her parents' views but had not developed her own to replace them);

c) the need for Dawn to remain in control of her life and Ron's role in helping her do this;

d) the marital relationship and, in particular, the respective gender roles.

As it turned out, because so much progress had been made between sessions 1 and 2, only two sessions were needed. The AMHP argued the case for holding the third session as planned in order to consolidate the gains made. Dawn and Ron, however, were adamant that this was not necessary.

These steps were successful in bringing Dawn out of her depression by establishing the balance she needed – the balance between being in control on the one hand, and being supported on the other. She commented that this was the first time she had achieved such a balance. Initially, her parents had been 'overcontrolling' and thus provided too much support, but when she left home she had regained control but felt isolated and unsupported.

Her marriage to Ron had brought her close to that balance but, as she had not shared her views about her parents with him, he had little understanding of her need for such balance. Indeed, until this crisis, Dawn had not articulated within her own mind her problems with her parents. She had just felt smothered and confused, and yet guilty, but did not understand why. The crisis intervention had taken her this major step forward.

The intervention was successful in a very short period of time and produced a very satisfactory and very rewarding end result – a clear example of the positive dimension of crisis.

The positive outcome was largely dependent on the assessment of the situation as a crisis, rather than as a medical problem requiring hospitalisation. Indeed, hospital admission could easily have compounded the problems.

The process of intervention was not without its problems, however. For example, the consultant psychiatrist, on learning that the recommendations for compulsory admission were not being effected, expressed considerable concern, questioned the AMHP's professional judgment and declared that the AMHP would be held personally responsible if Dawn were to harm herself or the child. The psychiatrist at this point gave the AMHP no opportunity to explain the rationale behind the intervention and was only marginally more willing to listen after the event.

Despite this lack of multidisciplinary understanding, crisis intervention had been very effective in empowering Dawn and had enabled her to swap hospital admission for the balanced life she sought.

iv) Discussion

Many of the characteristics of crisis intervention were visible in this case. Again, the subjective dimension was important, control played a central part and empowerment was a central aim. It was, in many ways, a classic example of crisis intervention, the disciplined use of crisis theory in an actual crisis situation.

A worker less attuned to crisis theory and its principles may have 'missed' the crisis nature of the situation and may thus have dealt with the case at face value by facilitating the admission to hospital of this 'sick' woman. The fact that there was a clear biological dimension to the situation (hormonal and other changes associated with childbirth) could easily have seduced the worker into perceiving it as a predominantly medical one and thus seeing hospitalisation as the logical solution.

The logic of crisis theory, as we have seen, leads to a very different solution. This does not mean that hospitalisation is never the solution, but it does mean that the implications of admitting a person in crisis to hospital must be very carefully thought through.

There were other significant aspects to this case – the part played by gender, for example. Whereas traditional crisis theory pays minimal attention to structural issues, such as class, race/ethnicity and gender, a modern anti-discriminatory form of crisis intervention needs to be sensitive to such issues and take them fully into account. Fortunately, in this case, both Dawn and Ron were receptive to discussing issues of gender and were able to recognise the part stereotypical gender expectations had played in the development of the crisis. Clients are, of course, not always so receptive, as the sexist assumptions that form a key part of patriarchal ideology run strong and deep. However, crisis is characteristically a time when people are more receptive to change than is generally the case.

Values also featured in this case scenario, in particular religious and moral values. One's values are an important source of support in times of stress – a degree of consistency and solidity when all else appears under threat. However, when it is one's values which are themselves under threat, the risk of crisis becomes significant.

In Dawn's case it was confusion over her values which had contributed to her being plunged into crisis. She felt she had not developed her own set of values – what values she had were largely a contradiction of her parents' values, a negative image of someone else's values rather than a positive set of her own.

The combination of the life crisis of childbirth (in which the responsibility for another human being raises value questions) and the re-imposition of her parents' influence (and thus values) was sufficient to plunge her into crisis, to overwhelm her coping resources. It was the meeting point of the existential dimension (values, meaning, identity, purpose) and the social dimension (power, influence, control, conflict). It was at this point that Dawn floundered but, through effective crisis intervention, was later empowered. She emerged from the crisis a far stronger person than when she had entered.

Case C

i) Scenario

Richard and Sue Parry presented themselves to the Community Drug and Alcohol Team on the recommendation of their GP who had recently become very concerned about Richard's excessive drinking and the effect this was having on the marital relationship.

The team was a small, multidisciplinary unit comprising a social worker, a community psychiatric nurse and a psychologist. They all had a high workload, but also shared a strong commitment to high standards of professional practice. Cases were sometimes dealt with jointly by two workers but, at the time of referral, work pressures prevented this happening in this case. The case was allocated to the least experienced member of the team who was supported by consultation with the other team members.

Richard and Sue were both in their early thirties, both in relatively well-paid employment with quite good prospects. They had both been married before and Sue had two children from her previous marriage. The foursome lived in a bungalow on an estate close to the city centre.

The couple had only been married a few months and, on assessment, the relationship appeared somewhat fragile and in need of consolidation. They recognised that they had reached crisis point – they could not cope with the situation as it was – and so they were keen to accept help and to co-operate with plans made.

ii) Assessment

The worker's assessment soon established that Richard's drinking had only become problematic in recent months. He had been a 'social drinker' since his late teens, but there had never been any concerns about the amount or frequency of his drinking.

The recent pattern, however, was doubly worrying in so far as consumption had increased significantly and had also become secretive. He had tried to conceal from Sue just how much he was drinking. Sue, however, realised all was not well; Richard's tendency to secretiveness implied a lack of trust and thus placed great strain on their relationship.

They realised this could not go on; the situation had become untenable and they felt desperate. Sue felt hopeful, but Richard felt helpless to change, but he did recognise that the problem was his to a large extent.

The worker set about looking for the trigger of the over-reliance on drink (based on the view that the problematic drinking was an attempted solution to an as yet unidentified problem – that is, the drinking was an unhelpful and destructive coping response). The aim was to identify the underlying factors so that intervention could be geared towards developing alternative, less destructive coping methods.

The couple had had no financial difficulties (although the excessive drinking was steadily changing this). Wider social issues did not appear to be major contributory factors in relation to the problems of this young, white, middle-class and non-disabled couple. However, on closer analysis, both class and gender did have parts to play.

A fragile relationship had been identified by the worker. Although now both 'professional' people, they had come from different class backgrounds with different habits and lifestyles. Their relationship was not sufficiently well established for them to have come to terms with the tensions and conflicts and to have reached a satisfactory compromise.

Gender issues were also a feature of the couple's circumstances. Sue's separation from her previous husband had been difficult and 'messy'. Sue still saw her husband at weekends when he picked up the children for access visits. This made for a tense and fraught situation, with confusion over roles and relationships.

Sue's method of coping with being trapped between two men was to become bad tempered and operate on a short fuse. Richard, by contrast, coped with what he saw as a competitive situation by withdrawing and, ultimately, drinking. The couple did not address the issues together, and so this lack of communication and sharing heightened the problems they were experiencing.

Richard had tried to be consistent and supportive in his relationship with Sue and the children, but he felt shut out, as if he had not been accepted and integrated into the family unit. The frequent contact between the children and their father reinforced Richard's feelings, and he had become terrified of rejection.

In a way, his drinking could be seen as a way of 'resigning before he was fired'. By withdrawing into drink, Richard was anaesthetising himself from his pain. But the drinking only added to the problems, and thus to the pain. The situation therefore became intolerable, and crisis point was reached – the point of no return, the critical moment when the relationship was on the point of breaking down.

iii) Intervention

In keeping with the time-limited nature of crisis intervention, it was agreed that the worker would offer the couple eight sessions in order to maximise the positive potential of the crisis by seeking to produce constructive change in the couple and their relationship.

The first two sessions were characterised by avoidance behaviour. Both somewhat defensive, Richard and Sue preferred to focus on the drinking and a strategy for reducing it, rather than the underlying problems. The issue of avoidance was therefore raised by the worker, as the drinking was itself a form of avoidance – an unhelpful coping method.

It became apparent that there was a double bind. After one 'failed' relationship it was important that Sue was not hurt again. She wanted Richard to take more responsibility to show how much he cared for her. However, the more he cared, the more she seemed to want to reject him (for fear of getting hurt again). They were stuck.

In the third and fourth sessions the barriers started to come down and the couple moved on quite markedly. It was at this stage that the issues of jealousy and the 'unfinished business' of the first relationship were recognised and confronted.

As a result of this, there was a further massive shift when they acknowledged that their attitude of 'the relationship has to succeed' was unhelpful and they began to confront more realistically the possibility of the relationship failing.

A further significant point to emerge was that of nonverbal communication. Richard needed continually to touch Sue as a way of making sure she still cared, and tended to follow her around. This annoyed and frustrated Sue who felt she had no space. Consequently, the worker set 'homework' – Sue was to be the one who did the touching, but only when she wanted to.

Sessions 5 and 6 represented a stage characterised by relief – Richard, because his need to be cared for was being met better, and Sue, because she felt more in control and less agitated.

This relief gave the couple the confidence to say what their needs were in the relationship and how and to what extent they could meet each other's needs. They were therefore able to work on a contract which negotiated how they could function better on a day-to-day basis.

This seemed to give them the space to talk more about Sue's previous relationship without Richard feeling too threatened.

The final two sessions were used to consolidate the progress made. They continued to test out their newly found freedom to feel safe enough to express their anxieties of being hurt again, but accepting that this was always a possibility. That is, they were learning to cope with the contingency of their relationship – and indeed of any relationship.

They acknowledged that there was still a lot of work to be done to secure their relationship. However, they now had a framework on which to build. They had been helped to gain the confidence they needed to undertake this work themselves without outside support – with the proviso of the safety net that further sessions could be arranged if needed.

By the final session, Richard's alcohol intake had decreased remarkably, as was confirmed by both partners. This was accompanied by a stronger relationship, increased coping abilities and an acute awareness that excessive drinking is more of a problem than a solution.

iv) Discussion

This was not a crisis characterised by panic and a sense of emergency. It was, none the less, a crisis situation. The couple's coping resources had been exhausted and they recognised they could not go on – the situation could only get drastically worse or drastically better. It was a challenge to the crisis worker to ensure that the latter was in fact the outcome – to use the energy and motivation generated by the crisis to turn threat into opportunity.

Where alcohol abuse in particular, or substance abuse in general, is considered, there is a need for very careful crisis assessment. This particular case was a genuine crisis, but often the artefacts of crisis are present – panic, confusion, a sense of urgency and desperation – when there is in fact no crisis. This is an example of 'furore', a state resembling crisis, but without the motivation to change, without having reached the critical moment, the point of no return. Furore is a coping method, a 'flustered' state that has the effect of attracting attention and support. It is generally an unhelpful coping method and may therefore result in a crisis in due course. However, it is not in itself a crisis.

This is similar to what had happened to Richard. When presented with stresses and problems, he used the refuge of drink as a way of coping – a destructive coping strategy which led to the crisis. The crisis worker's task, as in so many cases (for example, child abuse), was to facilitate the development of more constructive coping methods and support systems and thus 'ease out' the more potentially disastrous responses.

The intervention succeeded in achieving this in a relatively short period of time. By having such a rapid impact, the intervention did not lead to the dependency associated with some forms of long-term work. Crisis intervention succeeded in empowering Richard and Sue to the extent that they had no further need for professional intervention. This avoidance of dependency was of particular importance in this case, as the danger here was that Richard would fall foul of another form of dependency – dependence on drink. This would surely have ruined their marriage and thus scarred Sue with another 'failed' relationship, thereby leaving both their lives in tatters.

As this case illustrates, the stakes crisis workers play for are high indeed, but so too are the potential rewards in terms of both client outcome and job satisfaction for the workers concerned.

Conclusion

These three case studies have, I hope, succeeded in their aim of giving the 'flavour' of crisis theory in action – crisis intervention in the context of contemporary practice in the helping professions.

Inevitably the case studies are not exhaustive accounts, and many aspects have had to be left out. It remains the case, however, that the cases depicted here reflect and illustrate many of the elements of an approach to practice based on crisis intervention.

The examples used here represent a fairly narrow range of practice scenarios to which crisis intervention is applicable. The number of situations which invite a crisis intervention approach are many and varied and it would be an error of major proportions to assume that crisis theory has only a limited range of application. There are many other situations where crisis intervention can be very useful, not least the following:

• Admitting an elderly person to residential care is compatible with the crisis approach. Such an admission represents a crisis, as it involves the client reaching a situation in which conventional coping resources have broken down and a major change is needed to remove the danger inherent in the situation. And, as experienced practitioners in this field know only too well, such an admission can be either a wondrous relief or 'the end of the road', thus representing both the opportunity and threat of crisis.

• A member of a youth offending team would have ample opportunity to use crisis intervention – for example, where a young offender faces a custodial sentence and is desperate to avoid 'being sent down'.

• Health care professionals seeking to persuade patients to refrain from health-harming behaviour (smoking, excessive drinking and so on) will be in a stronger position to bring about such change at a time of crisis, in contrast to the resistance that is likely to feature strongly when the patient is in the relative comfort of homeostasis.

The case examples given in this chapter are illustrations of the successful use of crisis intervention, but of course there is by no means any guarantee that success will be achieved. There are many factors that may lead to failure; it is important to recognise that crisis intervention is not a 'magic box' to cure all ills.

Of course, these case studies are not intended as formulas to be followed or as 'model answers'. Effective crisis work is premised on a good understanding of the principles of crisis theory, the development of skills of crisis assessment and intervention and a sensitivity to the common pitfalls to be avoided. Following a formula is therefore not enough. However, it is to be hoped that these case studies can make a contribution to the development of reflective practice.

Points to ponder

> ➤ What would have happened in each of the three cases if there had been no intervention in the crises?
> ➤ What other examples of crisis might occur in people's lives that could come to your attention in your line of work?
> ➤ How important do you think teamwork is in crisis intervention?

Chapter 6
Exploring the Implications

Introduction

We have seen that crisis intervention can be a very effective and rewarding form of practice. However, we have also seen that it can be a very demanding and potentially dangerous undertaking. This raises a number of considerations which should be taken into account. In this chapter I shall address, in turn, what I see as the five most salient ones, although it has to be recognised that these are not the only ones.

Dealing with aggression and violence

People in crisis can at times be unpredictable and volatile. Consequently, we need to be conscious of the risk of violence, especially in situations where the crisis worker can be seen by the client(s) as 'the enemy' as a result of a combination of their role (in child protection or statutory mental health, for example) and the high level of emotion generated by the crisis.

Clients in crisis may feel threatened and vulnerable as a result of the loss which plunged them into crisis and may feel they have nothing further to lose in lashing out. There are numerous cases on record of clients attacking and harming professional helpers (see, for example, Newhill, 2004).

It was argued in Chapter 1 that it is important to see crises in their wider social and political context rather than simply as psychological issues. It is important, therefore, not to see violence as an individual, psychological matter but rather a wider concern. In keeping with the emphasis on a psychosocial approach, it is important to recognise that there will be significant sociological factors associated with aggression and violence. We therefore have to understand the social context in which actual or potential violence becomes a significant issue, rather than restrict ourselves to focusing on individual psychological factors.

The 'crisis matrix' – the various psychological, cultural, structural and existential factors which contribute to the crisis situation – is to be seen as an important element in our understanding and prediction of violence and our response to it. It is more appropriate to see violence as a characteristic of situations rather than simply of individuals. The circumstances in which interactions take place are ikely to be just as significant as the psychology of the individuals concerned if not more so.

My intention here is not to be alarmist or pessimistic. However, it would be both naive and unfair to paint a picture of crisis intervention which does not acknowledge the risk of aggression or violence. This risk is a fact of life for crisis workers.

It is, however, precisely that – a risk, and by no means a certainty. The majority of crisis intervention situations are managed without even a hint of violence and aggression. It is important to put the risk of violence into perspective. Violence is most certainly not a constant characteristic of crisis intervention, far from it, but the risk is none the less very real; the threat is always there. It therefore pays to be aware of the risk and be adequately prepared both to prevent aggression overspilling into actual violence and to respond as effectively as possible if it does.

It should be remembered that, while it makes sense for practitioners to be well informed on such issues, the responsibility for coping with client violence lies ultimately with the employing organisation. Crisis workers are not paid to be attacked. Their employers have a duty to protect them as far as possible and to provide maximum support where such protection fails. This is a significant health and safety concern.

The impact of threat and violence is a major issue to which we shall return below, under the heading of 'Supervision'. Dealing with such matters is an important, if not essential, part of an employing organisation's policy and practice of 'staff care' and commitment to workplace well-being.

Stress management

The Health and Safety Executive define stress as: 'The adverse reaction people have to excessive pressures or other types of demand placed on them at work' (www.hse.gov.uk/stress/furtheradvice/whatisstress.htm). Responding to other people's crises can place tremendous pressure on professional helpers in a variety of ways:

- aggression or violence (as discussed above);
- feelings of helplessness and powerlessness in the face of overwhelming suffering on the part of a client or clients (for example, after a bereavement);
- dealing with intense, raw emotion and extremes of distress (for example, removing a child from home on child protection grounds);
- unrealistic expectations from clients who see the practitioner as the route to salvation (see Raphael's discussion of role stereotypes: Raphael, 1990, p. 10);

- time pressures – other cases and duties do not disappear while the worker is immersed in a client crisis;
- crisis is characterised by risk and uncertainty and the crisis worker carries considerable responsibility for the outcome of the crisis (for example, approved mental health professional assessments).

This is not an exhaustive list but should be sufficient to depict the range of pressures associated with crisis intervention that may overspill into stress at times.

But pressure is only one component in the complex phenomenon of stress. Another important aspect is that of 'coping resources', the skills, strategies and methods we develop to help us manage the many and varied pressures to which we are exposed. We each have our 'repertoire' of such resources and there are two particular aspects of these coping resources which merit our attention:

i) Range

The wider one's range of coping mechanisms, the more 'insulated' one is from stress. Where we have only a small number of such resources, we may be vulnerable to being overwhelmed by the pressures.

The range of resources within a person's repertoire can vary significantly. Some people have an extensive repertoire of means of handling pressure – sport, humour, hobbies, a good social life and so on – while others may rely on a much narrower range (see the discussion referred to earlier of 'social capital').

ii) Suitability

Coping methods vary in their effectiveness, their timeliness and their 'side effects' – in short, their suitability for the situation at hand. A method may be suitable at some times but not at others – for example, humour. Joking at a time of crisis may be helpful or may stoke up the pressures even further. Such situations need to be carefully and sensitively appraised.

Some methods are effective in the short term but may prove detrimental in the longer term. For example, if we deny a problem exists, we are shielded from its pressures for the time being but, in the long run, the fact that we have denied the problem may mean that the pressures increase and multiply until we are forced to abandon denial and confront the problem's existence. In fact, this may actually be crisis point, the time when existing coping methods are ineffective and a new approach needs to be adopted.

Crisis workers, in recognition of the highly pressurised nature of the work, need to be aware of their own repertoire of coping methods and will need to ask themselves two questions of major importance:

1. Is the range of my coping repertoire sufficiently wide and well developed to protect me from the pressures of undertaking crisis intervention work?
2. Does my repertoire contain unhelpful or potentially damaging coping methods (for example, denial, aggression, excessive drinking)?

If the answer to question 1 is no, then care must be taken to extend and strengthen that repertoire. Similarly, if the answer to question 2 is yes, then steps to eliminate or reduce these should be taken so that they can be replaced by more helpful and constructive methods.

One useful step towards achieving the aim of a stronger repertoire is to list or 'brainstorm' the components of one's repertoire and determine which are particularly useful and worthy of nurturance, and which are potentially problematic. If this is done as a group exercise, workers can learn from each other and perhaps identify gaps in their range of resources and pick up useful tips for modifying, extending and improving their repertoire.

The third major component of stress management is that of support, or more specifically, support systems. How well people cope with pressure is not simply a matter of coping methods. It is not simply degree of pressure vying with degree of coping ability. The 'intervening variable' of support plays a major part.

Support systems are of two types, formal and informal. Formal support will be discussed below under the heading of 'Supervision'; I shall restrict myself here to a consideration of informal support.

Informal support exists both inside and outside work and derives from family, friends, colleagues and other social contacts. It plays a significant role in reducing pressure and reinforcing and boosting coping methods. A crisis situation can prove to be a very destabilising experience which unsettles the crisis worker and places a heavy burden on his or her coping resources. Good support is necessary to ensure that the pressure does not overpower the coping resources and produce a breakdown in homeostasis – that is, a crisis. Good support has the effect of reducing the impact of the pressure and of reinforcing the potency of coping resources. This can be illustrated in diagram form in Figure 7 (overleaf).

As with coping methods, there are two important questions for crisis workers to ask themselves in relation to support:

1. Am I receiving sufficient formal support (supervision, consultation, debriefing, training and so on) to help me cope with the pressures of crisis intervention?
2. Do I have access to sufficient informal support (family, friends and so on) to supplement and complement the formal support available?

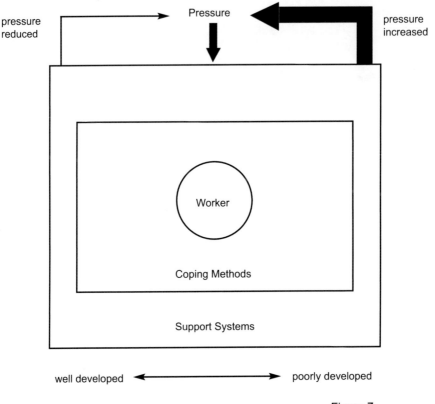

Figure 7:
Managing Pressure

Where gaps in support are identified, these can be seen as potential weak spots, possible danger signs which should prompt us to take steps to rectify the problem. As I shall argue below, managers have considerable responsibility for ensuring adequate formal support is provided for crisis workers. Informal support, however, is something practitioners of crisis intervention will need to organise for themselves.

In sum, stress management consists of three key elements:

• 'stressors', the inevitable pressures of crisis work;
• coping resources, strategies for managing pressure and resisting stress;
• support systems, the emotional and practical 'back up' needed.

Professional helpers involved in crisis intervention would be foolish to ignore these issues. Indeed, crisis workers who take no account of stress management place themselves at risk – an additional and unnecessary risk.

The abuse of power

In Chapter 8 we will explore the significance of power and empowerment and will recognise that crisis situations are characterised by the potential for the abuse or misuse of power. We must therefore be very careful to ensure that we do not fall into the trap of allowing crisis pressures to lead us into unethical or counterproductive behaviour.

Supervision

Crisis intervention has implications for the nature of supervision and the supervisory relationship. As we have seen, crisis work can make major demands on practitioners in terms of time, emotion, commitment and judgment. Supportive supervision should therefore be an important resource for crisis workers to draw upon. Consequently, it would be helpful to outline what this entails.

One of the tasks of supervision is the provision of assistance and guidance in workload management – to advise on setting priorities and preventing excessive workload demands. This task is of particular value for staff undertaking crisis ntervention because of the intensive time demands of crisis work. Crises do not fit neatly into office hours or in between meetings and appointments. A great deal of flexibility is required and the manager with supervisory responsibility can be called upon to play a significant part in facilitating this.

One of the dangers of poor supervision is that a supervisor who is insensitive to (or unaware of) the demands of crisis intervention is likely to add to the pressures rather than subtract from them. It is therefore important for supervisors (and indeed other managers) to have a good understanding of crisis theory and the principles and realities of crisis intervention.

The pressurised and emotionally demanding nature of crisis work can lead to poor decision making, unwise moves and a potentially disastrous impact on clients. This is one of the risks of crisis work; those who are brave enough to undertake it deserve the 'safety net' benefit of effective supervision.

This aspect of the team leader's role acts as a support function for staff. However, there are other support functions which also need to be borne in mind. For example, reference was made earlier to the role of formal support in relation to stress management. Such formal support has a number of dimensions as follows:

- Shared accountability for work undertaken (thus sharing the pressure to a certain extent).
- The opportunity for constructive release of the intense feelings which can be generated by crisis work.
- Appraisal of performance – constructive feedback on strengths and weaknesses to facilitate professional development and improved morale.
- Team building – helping to provide a supportive peer group and environment.

These are tasks which should perhaps be undertaken in any well-run team in the helping professions but, for a team in which crisis intervention is taken seriously, these tasks are key elements in the framework of support. They are an essential component of the support system that gives crisis workers the confidence to tackle crises positively and constructively.

Service delivery systems

Every service provision organisation has a system and set of procedures for dealing with new referrals. As with most types of system, there is considerable variation in the efficiency, responsiveness and effectiveness among the different systems in use. As crisis intervention is premised on a fast response to ensure maximum therapeutic value, the system's capability for responding speedily is a crucial feature.

A well-oiled, carefully thought-out referral management system run by committed and experienced staff can also provide the organisational context needed to facilitate crisis work. My aim, therefore, is not to prescribe which system of responding to referrals should be used. Rather, my intention is to advocate that, whatever system is in use, sufficient flexibility and responsiveness must be built in to that system to promote, rather than prohibit, good crisis work.

However, we should not allow the emphasis here on initial referral work to mislead us into the false assumption that crisis intervention is not applicable to longer-term cases.

Long-standing cases also produce crises and can be amenable to crisis intervention techniques. The service delivery system in which this work takes place should therefore be organised in such a way as to permit, facilitate and encourage the use of crisis intervention.

One aspect of this is the promotion of good teamwork. To allow the flexibility crisis intervention demands, it is helpful for team members to be aware of each other's cases, in outline at least, so that the team can be supportive in dealing with routine work while a particular team member is engrossed in a crisis situation.

One aspect of the organisational context which can help to facilitate this is a 'pairing' arrangement. Each worker 'teams up' with a colleague and they keep each other briefed on developments in their respective cases. This has three distinct advantages:

1. If a crisis arises while the practitioner concerned is not available, his or her partner will be in a more informed position to respond.
2. As mentioned above, a partner can help cope with the work left behind when a crisis makes sudden and intense demands on our time.
3. Pressures and responsibilities are shared by, for example, joint visits or case discussions.

This is only one suggestion amongst many organisational variables which could possibly be changed or adjusted in order to provide a sound organisational context from which to undertake crisis intervention. Crisis work is difficult and demanding enough without having to swim against the tide of the organisational context or culture.

Conclusion

This chapter has summarised some key issues that can be seen to set the scene for addressing the implications of drawing on crisis theory in practice. By no means all of the implications have been tackled, but I hope that enough has been covered to set in motion the type of planning that has to take place if the major benefits of crisis theory are to be optimally translated into the reality of day-to-day professional practice across the helping professions.

This chapter now concludes Part Two, with its focus on actual practice, but this does not mean that we have exhausted the subject of practice, as the discussions in Part Three about the underpinning values of crisis intervention are also highly relevant to practice, and so it is to this topic that we now turn.

Points to ponder

> ➤ What steps can you take to minimise the risk of aggression or violence occurring in a crisis situation?
> ➤ What strategies can you draw on to prevent crisis situations becoming stressful for you?
> ➤ How can you help your supervisor to be as supportive of you as possible?

Part Three: Tackling Discrimination and Oppression

Introduction

Part Three contains two chapters, both of which are concerned with the importance of making sure that the pressures of the crisis situation do not allow us to lose sight of the need to tackle discrimination and oppression. In the first we focus on the overall picture of how crisis intervention needs to be sensitive to the potential for discrimination, to prevent it where possible and to respond appropriately when it does arise. This chapter fits well with the recurring theme throughout the book of the need for our practice to be based on a psychosocial approach – that is, one that takes account of sociological factors as well as psychological ones.

The second chapter focuses more specifically on empowerment. This is a very important chapter to end with, as empowerment is at the heart of crisis intervention. Oversimplified approaches to crisis that simply seek to return the client to a pre-crisis state of homeostasis miss significant opportunities for people to grow and develop, to become stronger, better equipped to deal with the next crisis and thus to have more control over their lives – which is precisely what empowerment is all about.

Chapter 7
Anti-discriminatory Practice

Introduction

In Chapter I, I was critical of the narrow individualistic focus of traditional crisis theory (what elsewhere I have referred to as an atomistic approach – Thompson, 2010) and its failure to appreciate the significance of wider social factors. This chapter builds on that critique by presenting arguments as to why it is important to understand crisis intervention more holistically and, in doing so, make it compatible with emancipatory approaches to practice – that is, practices that challenge discrimination and oppression. In doing this I am building on my earlier work in this field (Thompson 2006a; 2007; 2011a).

For some time now there has been an increasing recognition of the need to take account of discrimination in people's lives. While the concerns that members of the helping professions encounter in their work clearly have a personal dimension specific to the individual(s) concerned, it would be a significant mistake to fail to recognise how wider social processes like exclusion, marginalisation, alienation and stereotyping can also be significant factors in shaping the problems people experience and how they respond to the challenges involved.

To discriminate literally means to identify a difference. However, its legal and moral sense goes a step beyond this to understand discrimination as a twofold process:

1. to identify a difference (for example, between social groups) and
2. to treat a group (or member of that group) unfairly as a result of that difference.

Racism is an example of discrimination. While there may well be differences between ethnic groups that can be identified, to assume that such differences justify minority groups being excluded, treated less favourably or otherwise treated badly reflects racist thinking. It involves moving (without justification) from discriminating between groups to discriminating against particular groups. Such discrimination then has the effect of oppressing those people who are on the receiving end of such unfair assumptions and treatment.

For a long time discrimination was conceptualised as personal prejudice and was therefore seen as primarily a matter of individual psychology. However, for some time now we have appreciated that discrimination is a psychosocial phenomenon and that it operates at personal, cultural and structural levels (see the Guide to Further Learning for details of literature about these complex issues). What this means is that an adequate understanding of discrimination needs to go beyond the individual level and take account of social factors, such as power relations (to be discussed further in Chapter 8). This chapter is therefore concerned with developing an understanding of the wider social context of crisis intervention so that issues of discrimination and oppression are not neglected.

The wider picture

Each of us is a unique individual in our own right, but we also need to recognise that we are unique individuals in a social context. Power and opportunities ('life chances' as the sociologist, Weber, called them) are not randomly distributed within society but are clearly linked to the structure of society. This relates to the major social divisions, such as class, race, gender, age and so on. All of these are relevant to how we may cope with crises. For example, class is a reflection of socio-economic position and this is, of course, a significant issue in relation to the availability of coping resources. Wealth and economic power do not guarantee an absence of crisis – far from it – but money can buy access to wider coping resources (for example, the services of a solicitor, private medicine, expensive holidays to relieve stress). Differences in access to resources in general can therefore be seen to parallel access to coping resources in particular.

Class-related factors, such as poverty and health, contribute not only to one's resourcefulness to respond to crises, but also one's vulnerability to crisis in the first place. The question of health inequalities is therefore an important factor. For example, research from the Joseph Rowntree Foundation (Mitchell *et al.*, 2000) found that approximately:

- 7,500 deaths among people younger than 65 could be prevented if inequalities in wealth were narrowed to their 1983 levels;
- 2,500 deaths per year amongst those aged less than 65 would be prevented if full employment could be achieved.
- 1,400 lives would be saved per year among those under 15 if child poverty were to be eradicated.

Class is therefore an important aspect of understanding the phenomena of crisis onset and crisis resolution.

Similarly, the structured inequalities associated with race/ethnicity can also play a significant part. Within Britain's multi-racial, multiethnic context, racism and its attendant inequalities and prejudices place greater social, economic and psychological pressures on black people and other ethnic minorities, and institutionalised racism limits their access to formal support systems.

Race and ethnicity should therefore be recognised as important aspects of the 'crisis matrix', the complex web of factors which contribute to the crisis scenario. Racism can be seen as a potential contributory factor in both the onset of crisis, as a result of the stresses and pressures it brings to bear, and the resolution of crisis, in terms of restricted access to institutional support networks (although the resilience of minority ethnic groups to 'bounce back' from such difficulties should not be underestimated).

Similarly, it has long been recognised that inequalities based on gender place an increased burden of coping on women. For example, as long ago as 1983 Finch and Groves pointed out that women are expected to be the main providers of care for children, elderly or disabled relatives. Thus Finch and Groves argue that community care is in fact family care which, in turn, amounts primarily to care by women. The burden of coping placed on women's shoulders is therefore a very heavy one.

This is only one example amongst many of extra pressures upon women as a result of the patriarchal ideology which operates in modern British society (see, for example Connell, 2002). Thus, women may be more vulnerable to crisis due to the oppressive nature of a society based on sexism. It has long been recognised that women's substance abuse (both illegal drugs and tranquillisers and so on) can be linked to the socially constructed dependency role women are expected to occupy: 'tranquilliser use in the private sphere may be, whether consciously or not, a housewife's only comfort and relief from stress' (Ettorre, 1989, p. 107).

Also, there is a significant body of research which establishes links between women and higher levels of depression (see, for example, Kessler, 2003). In a classic study Brown and Harris (1978) identified that factors such as lack of outlet from the domestic sphere, relative isolation and lack of emotional support were found to be strongly associated with depression and these, in turn, are associated with the circumstances of women in modern Britain.

In sum, therefore, traditional crisis theory can be criticised for adopting a predominantly white, middle-class, male perspective on a range of issues which relate very closely to structured inequalities and the oppressive social divisions which stack the odds against certain groups in society. An understanding of social disadvantage and discrimination must be incorporated into the theoretical framework if a new crisis theory is to replace the old and thereby make a contribution to anti-discriminatory practice.

Furthermore, the major social divisions of class, race and gender are not the only ones which need to be considered. Age, disability and sexual orientation are also relevant factors, as indeed are any other forms of discrimination and disadvantage.

One of the main reasons for traditional crisis theory's blindness to these structural factors is the model of society which it uses as its baseline, namely what sociologists would call a 'consensus' or 'order' model (Mullaly, 2002). This model assumes that there are no fundamental conflicts of interest within society and that whatever conflicts do occur are peripheral to the underlying consensus of what is presented as a basically homogeneous society. This somewhat naive model needs to be replaced with a more sophisticated 'conflict' one which addresses, and takes account of, the conflicts of class, race and gender and so on, which are part and parcel of the structure of society, for such conflicts circumscribe the situations in which crises occur and structure the coping resources available and are thus important dimensions of crisis intervention.

Another major weakness of crisis intervention which flows from this consensus model is its use of the now somewhat outmoded notion of 'adjustment'. Words such as 'maladaptive' are frequently employed to indicate unsuccessful or unhelpful behaviours. This is suggestive of someone who fails to fit in with social expectations, someone who is unable or unwilling to conform to standardised views of appropriate behaviour. The problem with this notion is that it 'pathologises' the person(s) concerned. It implies that the problem underlying the crisis is a 'failure of adjustment' and thus lays the blame for the situation on the individual(s) experiencing the crisis. This is a 'reductionist' approach, in so far as it reduces a complex psychosocial situation to a straightforward matter of pathology, of individual failing.

Clearly this involves a value judgment which could act as a barrier to therapeutic progress. A more appropriate and less judgmental concept is that of 'empowerment'. As we shall discuss in more detail in Chapter 8, the task of the crisis worker is to help empower people to take greater control of their circumstances and thus be better equipped to handle future crises – to be in a more powerful position (Thompson, 2007). The notion of 'adjustment' implies that changes need to be internal, psychological ones, whereas empowerment is a more global concept, encompassing both internal, personal power (for example, control of emotions, ability to resist panic) and wider power issues relating to social circumstances (for example, a woman obtaining an injunction against a violent partner).

If the crisis worker is to seek empowerment rather than adjustment, this entails not simply interventions geared towards coping skills, but also advocacy and other such ways of tackling the 'external' as well as internal factors. This involves taking a wider perspective than a clinical casework approach and thus taking account of social, as well as individual or familial factors.

The challenges of practice

Having an understanding of how discrimination and oppression work in society is a good starting point. However, there remain some significant challenges in drawing on such an understanding in our actual practice, especially in pressurised crisis situations.

The wider the focus the worker takes, the smaller the impact he or she can have upon the factors identified. The narrower, more individualistic the focus, the greater the impact the worker can have in terms of power, influence and access to resources. This, however, should not be used as an excuse for not attempting to influence or change the wider social issues or, indeed, to incorporate them into our assessment of the situations we encounter.

Taking anti-discriminatory practice seriously involves a wide range of steps, not least the following:

- Not focusing narrowly on the individual in isolation; taking account of their 'social location' – how they fit into the wider social sphere.
- Considering whether and how processes of discrimination may be:
    - Contributing to the crisis situation as precipitating factors or at least factors that exacerbate the situation;
    - Acting as a barrier to coping or blocking access to sources of support.
- Weighing up how the worker-client dynamics may be affected by social factors (for example, a male helper with a female client or vice versa, a white helper with a black client and so on).
- Exploring possible sources of help based on social factors (access to a women's empowerment group or a black support group in the community, for example).

Given the complexities involved, there can be no simple, formulaic approach to how to 'do' anti-discriminatory practice. It is more a case of practising within a set of values that promote equality and diversity and reject the unfairness and indignity on which discrimination is based. It amounts to developing what has come to be known as critically reflective practice (Thompson and Thompson, 2008a) – that is, well-informed, carefully thought-out practice that is attuned to the need to take account of the wider social context as well as the specifics of the individual and family situation.

One vitally important aspect of this situation to consider is the significance of the fact that so much discrimination is unintentional, based on a lack of awareness rather than malice. This has significant implications for how we practise. This is because, if we assume that discrimination is predominantly intentional, then we may assume that our own well-intentioned actions are not discriminatory.

However, it is important to realise that, because discrimination is not simply a matter of prejudice, our actions may reflect cultural and structural aspects of discrimination. Consider the following examples:

- Reinforcing traditional gender roles by assuming that the man in a family is the breadwinner or that the woman has primary responsibility for child care.
- Alienating black people by not taking account of cultural differences or needs.
- Assuming that an elderly person is not capable of making a decision for him- or herself.

Sadly, these are not uncommon occurrences due to the powerful influences of our cultural upbringing. This is not intended as a personal criticism of individuals, but rather a recognition of how deeply ingrained discrimination is in our society. What is needed, then, is what Leonard (1997) calls critical self-reflection. Mullaly (2002) explains this as follows:

> Because we all internalize to varying degrees parts of the dominant ideology, it is important to develop reflexive knowledge of the dominant ideology to see how it constrains us and limits our freedom. Reflexive knowledge, derived mainly through critical self-reflection, is knowledge about ourselves. It helps us understand how ... we may exercise power in our professional and personal lives to either reproduce or resist social features that limit others' agency. (p. 207)

This can be challenging enough in everyday circumstances, but is likely to be even more demanding in a crisis situation. It is therefore important that, in engaging in crisis work, we go in well equipped in terms of having the necessary knowledge and understanding of the complexities of discrimination in order to try and ensure that our practice is genuinely anti-discriminatory practice (see the Guide to Further Learning for details of relevant texts to assist with this).

Conclusion

People experiencing a crisis can be very vulnerable and relatively powerless, and therefore liable to exploitation. It is therefore important that professional helpers use their power in such circumstances to help them move forward positively and to be especially careful not to reinforce discrimination and oppression. This, as we have seen, is not a straightforward matter, but it should also be clear that the efforts involved in developing our knowledge, skills and confidence in this area of professional practice are well worth it in terms of the dangers to be averted and the benefits to be achieved.

A key part of anti-discriminatory practice is a focus on empowerment, helping people gain greater control over their lives in various ways, including removing or minimising the obstacles that discrimination puts in place. For this reason Chapter 8 addresses the significance of empowerment for crisis intervention.

Points to ponder

> ➤ Why might discrimination be more of an issue in a crisis situation?
> ➤ Why is it important not to 'pathologise' people in crisis?
> ➤ How can you make sure that the pressures of the crisis situation do not lead you into a situation where you might be discriminating (perhaps even without realising that you are doing so)?

Chapter 8
Empowerment

Introduction

Chapter 7 made it clear that crisis situations are very significant when it comes to anti-discriminatory practice, as the unsettled and pressurised nature of such situations can allow discrimination to feature – for example, by relying on stereotypes in the heat of the moment, rather than assessing situations properly, or by making unwarranted assumptions. This chapter takes these issues a step further by exploring the significance of empowerment.

On a negative note, crisis situations are quite challenging, as they can be very problematic in terms of discrimination and oppression as a result of the vulnerability and insecurity that are so common at times of major upheaval. However, on a more positive note, crises offer excellent scope for empowerment. As we shall explore in more detail below, the energy created by a crisis can free people up to move forward in ways that they would have been reluctant to do while in the relative security of homeostasis.

The chapter is divided into two main parts. In the first we explore the significance of power and powerlessness in crisis situations, and in the second we consider how empowerment can become a strong feature of our crisis intervention work.

Power and powerlessness

Power is a widely used but commonly misunderstood or oversimplified term. Space does not permit a detailed exploration of the complexities involved, but, for present purposes, it should be noted that there are different types and levels of power and that it is not simply a matter of there being two types of people, the powerful and the powerless (see Thompson, 2007, for a fuller account). It is also important to note that power is not necessarily a problem; in fact, the ethical and appropriate use of power can be a major asset in helping people in difficult and distressing circumstances. The real challenge comes in being able to use power constructively to help clients to develop greater control over their lives and circumstances, rather than use our power against clients' interests for our own ends or to solve our own problems. Consider the following two scenarios:

Scenario A

Marie was devastated when she discovered that her 15-year-old son, Sean, had been arrested for possession of Class A drugs. She knew that he had been having difficulties at school, and that she had found it difficult to control him at home, but she was shocked to find that his troubles had gone this far. At first she was reluctant to accept help from the youth offending team, but in desperation and not knowing what else to do, she agreed to receive help. This proved to be a turning point for Marie, as the support she received helped her to make changes at home and in her relationship with Sean. Since her husband had left almost two years before she had been on the verge of depression and had not really got close to Sean or helped him to deal with his feelings of loss at the departure of his father. As a result of the help the family received, Marie felt stronger and more in control, with a fuller understanding of how she needed to do some active parenting of Sean rather than just leave him to his own devices. Sean too benefitted by feeling more secure at home and by having clearer boundaries. The youth offending team members involved had used their power to help Marie and Sean have greater control over their lives and problems – they had helped them move forward constructively, using their power positively to create positive power for Marie and Sean.

Scenario B

Sîan was a community nurse in a rural area. She had been involved for a while with Mrs Ferguson, a 79-year-old woman who had very mild confusion. Mrs Ferguson's daughter and son-in-law had referred her to the local community services department as they felt she should be in residential care. A social worker had visited but had come to the conclusion that residential care was not necessary. Mrs Ferguson's relatives were not happy with this and put Sîan and the social worker under a great deal of pressure to arrange residential care. They phoned them both constantly and made comments like: 'If anything happens to her, it will be your fault' and they threatened to go to the newspapers to expose their 'uncaring' approach and their 'negligence'. As a result of this pressure Sîan and the social worker visited Mrs Ferguson and tried to persuade her to accept a place in residential care, at least on a short-term basis. They both realised that this was a potentially problematic way of dealing with the situation and felt uncomfortable with their approach. However, both professionals were relatively inexperienced and were receiving little support from their respective employing organisations. This was not a crisis for Mrs Ferguson, but it was for the professionals as they did not know how to cope with it. Despite their attempts to persuade her, Mrs Ferguson stood her ground. She used her own personal power to challenge the illegitimate use of professional power. What it boiled down to was that the relatives were using their power inappropriately to try and persuade the professionals to act unethically. Instead of the two professionals using their power to resist the relatives' power moves, they gave into them and thereby ended up using their power illegitimately too. Thankfully, Mrs Ferguson's power to say no, despite pressure, prevented this situation from getting even worse.

One of the clear implications of these contrasting scenarios is that professionals need to develop the knowledge, skills and confidence to be able to use their power ethically and constructively, especially in difficult situations like crises, whether a crisis for the client or for the worker. To neglect the power dimension of our work can therefore be a very serious mistake.

The situations that lead to the use of crisis intervention generally involve the coming together of vulnerable and relatively powerless clients who, by virtue of being in crisis, are often at their weakest, and relatively powerful professional helpers. Crisis workers are powerful in the following ways:

- we possess specialist knowledge and expertise;
- we may have access to, and control over, resources;
- we may exercise some degree of influence over other agencies;
- we have the power to offer support conditionally;
- we have the power to 'close the case' and withdraw support; but, perhaps most of all:
- clients place their faith and trust in us.

Where there is power, there is of course also the risk of the abuse or misuse of power. This is especially the case where such power derives from social divisions such as gender, race/ethnicity and age, as these power relations are institutionalised – they are 'built-in' to our everyday thinking and often go unquestioned (Lukes, 2005).

Self-awareness can be seen as an important part of critically reflective practice in general and therefore a significant aspect of crisis intervention in particular. However, I would wish to extend this to incorporate social awareness – that is, awareness of one's social location and the significance of this in terms of power relations. Going about our business without considering the role of power is dangerous enough in ordinary circumstances, but in a crisis situation, the results could be disastrous for all concerned.

If we are to avoid misusing power, it is necessary to be aware of what power we have – in terms of the factors listed above (those deriving from professional status), plus those deriving from one's social location (for example, the power of men in a patriarchal society – Westwood, 2002).

Caplan, one of the early pioneers of crisis intervention, made the point that: 'Crisis ... presents care-giving persons with a remarkable opportunity to deploy their efforts to maximum advantage in influencing the mental health of others' (1964, p. 54). We need to be clear that 'influence' is closely related to power. It is a relatively small step from influencing clients to controlling them. Establishing control is a key part of crisis situations, but this refers to taking control of the situation in partnership, rather than taking control of clients. Of course, there are situations in which control of clients is quite legitimately exercised – for example, via court orders – but this should only occur in clearly defined circumstances and only where necessary.

There is a subtle but significant difference between exercising legitimate authority on the one hand and, on the other, taking advantage of people rendered vulnerable by crisis to manipulate the situation to one's own advantage.

This is a complex area with no simple solutions or formulaic ways forward. Influence, control and power are common ingredients of crisis intervention. They can be used positively – within a non-judgmental, anti-discriminatory framework – or they can be abused and exploited, especially in the heat of crisis. One of the implications of adopting a crisis intervention approach is therefore the need to understand, appreciate and guard against the potential for the abuse or misuse of power.

Empowerment in crisis situations

If, then, we are to not only guard against negative uses of power, but also go so far as to use power positively to help others develop their power, what do we need to do? What steps do we need to take? Once again, there are no simple ways forward. We are again in the realm of critically reflective practice which involves having to weigh up situations carefully, drawing on our professional knowledge base, rather than looking for simple recipes for practice. However, there are some guidelines that can help us move forward, including the following:

- *Create a sense of security* Crises will often generate a strong sense of insecurity because of the destabilisation involved. Professional helpers can support progress by offering general reassurance (but not false reassurance) and support, as well as helping with specific points of concern that are contributing to the sense of insecurity. This can be difficult at first, especially for inexperienced workers, but it is important to develop the skills involved. In some respects these are basic inter-personal skills widely used in the helping professions, but in a crisis situation we may need to take them to a higher, more advanced level if we are to be effective in putting people at their ease when they are perhaps distressed, anxious and feeling threatened. A key part of this is the effective use of body language. If we are ex pressing our own anxiety, uncertainty and lack of confidence through our nonverbal communication, then we may actually be adding to the sense of insecurity rather than alleviating it.

• *Explore options* People in crisis may feel hopeless and helpless, believing there is no way out of their predicament. Added to this may be a fear of making the situation worse. Difficulty in thinking clearly because of the emotional pressures involved can also be part of the mix. This combination can lead to a dead end if we are not careful. The positive energy and motivation generated by the crisis can be blocked by these factors Reassurance, as mentioned above, can be helpful, but this needs to be supplemented with the exploration of options. Helping the person(s) concerned to identify the range of possible ways forward and to evaluate them in terms of the pluses and minuses, the potential benefits and the risks involved. This can be beneficial in three ways:

1. By providing a focus and structure, we are not only adding to the sense of security, but also providing a helpful framework to work to;
2. By working together on the options a partnership approach and sense of solidarity can be developed (see the discussion of 'connections' below); and
3. The exploration of options can potentially identify one or more ways forward that may appeal to, or capture the imagination of, the client.

• *Explore barriers to progress* Barriers to progress can be real or imagined (through fear and uncertainty). Empowerment can be promoted by identifying the various barriers to progress and dividing them into subjective and objective:
  – *Subjective* These are barriers based on how the situation is perceived. Such perceptions may be accurate and realistic or they may be distorted by the anxiety and insecurity of the crisis situation (for example, confidence being undermined by a temporary lack of self-belief). The professional helper can play a valuable role by helping to clear up the distortions and think about how to address the concerns that remain.
  – *Objective* These are barriers that exist beyond the individual: a lack of resources; other people's attitudes and so on. Here the helper can be supportive by assisting the client in exploring options for addressing these problems. Sometimes just knowing that they are not alone in

dealing with these challenges can be a huge source of personal strength and thus potential empowerment.

- *Look for connections* The point was made in Part One that it is important to move beyond the narrow, psychological focus of traditional crisis theory and to incorporate social elements into our work. This is a good example of how this applies. Empowerment can be promoted not just by working with the client in isolation, but also by helping them to 'connect' with other people – whether within their own informal network of contacts or through support groups and other such potential sources of social support. This links with the important notion of 'social capital' discussed earlier (Castiglione *et al.*, 2008). Just as people differ in their possession or otherwise of financial capital, there will be differences in social capital for individuals and groups – that is, differences in social resources that they can draw on. For those people who are high on social capital, the task may be a relatively simple one of helping them draw on those resources. For people low on social capital (because of long-term mental health problems, for example), the task may be much more complex and demanding and involve trying to develop relevant social resources rather than just 'plugging in' to existing ones.
- *Consolidate gains* Crisis situations can be tense and fraught with difficulties, and so it is possible for gains made to be lost – for example, for confidence to grow, but then to recede again because of a setback. This then raises the question of the need to consolidate the gains made – that is, to strengthen them wherever possible. To do this we need to be clear about what those gains have been, to review progress. This in itself can be empowering, as the client may be so engrossed in the demands of the situation that he or she fails to recognise the positive steps made.
- *Reinforce the three Rs* In an earlier work (Thompson, 2009c) I emphasised the importance of the three Rs:
  - *Resourcefulness* This refers to the ability to be creative in our problem-solving efforts and not to rely on a small repertoire of methods or steps.
  - *Robustness* This relates to our ability to withstand pressure, to remain positive and constructive despite various obstacles and discouragements.
  - *Resilience* Here the emphasis is on our ability to bounce back from adversity, to 'get over' setbacks and to recover as soon as reasonably possible.

These can be seen to be doubly important, as they are both what crisis workers need and what we need to instil (and/or build on) in the people we are helping, as far as we can. Whatever steps we can take toward reinforcing these three Rs (in ourselves and in the people we are seeking to help) will be steps towards empowerment.

This is not an exhaustive account of what can be done to promote empowerment in crisis situations, but it should be enough to lay down a platform from which further learning and understanding can be developed.

Conclusion

A crisis is a turning point, a situation which can get better or worse but which, by definition, will not stay the same. When it comes to issues of power and empowerment this is a very important point to remember. In such unsettled circumstances our actions (and therefore our exercise of power) can be positive or negative, empowering or disempowering, in effect either making the situation better or making it worse. It is to be hoped that this brief discussion of power and empowerment will therefore play an important part in raising awareness of how 'tuned in' we need to be to the operation of power in crisis situations if we are to ensure that our input is helpful and empowering rather than unhelpful and potentially oppressive.

Points to ponder

> ➢ Why is power an important issue in crisis situations?
> ➢ What power do you have as a professional worker?
> ➢ How can you use your power to help empower others?

Introduction

The *Theory into Practice* series is intended to provide introductory texts that provide a gateway to the wider and more advanced literature and to other sources of knowledge and understanding available. Part Four therefore comprises a set of suggestions for taking your understanding further. It is divided into three sections: books; journals; and organisations and internet resources. You are strongly encouraged to make full use of this guide, as it is important to develop a fuller basis of understanding. As we have seen, crisis intervention is a complex and demanding approach. It is therefore wise to build up as good a foundation of knowledge and understanding as we can to help us to be as fully equipped for rising to the challenges involved as we reasonably can be. Please do not make the mistake of assuming that a basic introductory book (whether this one or any other) is enough in itself to provide all that you need to know. Any introductory book should be seen as part of a process of developing the knowledge and understanding you need, but it is only part of that process – a beginning or a next step, but certainly not the end.

Books

Crisis intervention generally

Basic introductions are to be found in Stepney and Ford (2000) and Thompson and Thompson (2008b). More detailed readings are to be found in Roberts (2005). Everstine and Everstine (2006) is also a very useful resource. Other texts worth reading are Aguilera (1998); Echterling *et al.* (2004); James (2000); Kanel (2006).

For literature relating to crisis intervention in disaster situations, see Raphael (1990) and Leach (1994) for classic works, and Lattanzi-Licht and Doka (2003) for a more recent treatment of the issues.

Pressure, stress and problem solving

My own work on stress is to be found in Thompson *et al.* (1996) and Thompson (1999), with some relevant chapters also in Thompson and Bates (2009). Other useful resources include: Cranwell-Ward and Abbey (2005); Palmer and Cooper (2007); and Sutherland and Cooper (2000). My work on problem solving more broadly is to be found in Thompson (2006b). See also Egan (2006).

Loss, grief and trauma

There is a vast literature relating to these areas. In relation to loss and grief, my own edited collection (Thompson, 2002) is a good starting point, but the following all have much to offer: Aries (1991); Attig, (1996; 2000); Berzoff and Silverman (2004); Corr *et al.* (2008); DeSpelder and Strickland (2007); Howarth (2007); Kellehear (2005); Klass *et al.* (1996); Neimeyer (2000; 2001).

In relation to trauma, the following are worth exploring: Bracken (2002); Brewin (2003); Calhoun and Tedeschi (1999); Harvey (2002); Herman (2001); Rosen (2004); Scott and Palmer (2000); Solomon and Siegel (2003); and Warren (2006). For an understanding of childhood trauma, see Tomlinson (2004); Tomlinson and Philpot (2008); Rose and Philpot (2005); and Rymaszewska and Philpot (2006). For an exploration of issues relating to loss, grief and trauma in the workplace, see Thompson (2009d).

Aggression and violence

The following offer a good basis for understanding: Booker (2004); Clark and Linsley (2006) and Cloke and Goldsmith (2005).

Other helping approaches

Several other approaches to helping have been mentioned in this book. To find out more about these, the following are good starting points:

- *Advocacy*: Bateman (2000);
- *Cognitive-behavioural work*: Westbrook *et al.* (2007);
- *Counselling*: McLeod (2009);
- *Groupwork*: Doel (2005);
- *Solution-focused work*: Myers (2007); and
- *Task-centred practice*: Marsh and Doel (2006).

Anti-discriminatory practice

My own work includes a basic introduction (Thompson, 2006a) and a more advanced text (Thompson, 2011a). Other general texts include: Moss (2007); Baxter (2001) and Baker et al. (2004).

There has also been a great deal written about specific areas of discrimination, and the following are good 'entry points' to the literature:

- *Ageism* Sue Thompson (2005);
- *Disablism* Swain *et al.* (2004);
- *Racism* Solomos (2003); and
- *Sexism* Cranny Francis *et al.* (2003);

Empowerment

My own views on this important topic are to be found in Thompson (2007). Other important texts include: Nolan *et al.* (2007); Adams (2008); Barnes and Bowl (2001) and Linhorst (2006).

Existentialism

I have written extensively about existentialism and social work (Thompson 1992; 2010), although much of what I have written is also applicable to the helping professions more broadly. For other insights into existentialism, see: Van Deurzen and Arnold-Baker (2005) and Appignanesi and Zarate (2006).

Journals

Crisis – The Journal of Crisis Intervention and Suicide Prevention
http://www.hhpub.com/journals/crisis/

Crisis Intervention and Time-Limited Treatment
http://www.ingentaconnect.com/content/tandf/gcit

Death Studies
http://www.tandf.co.uk/journals/titles/07481187.asp

Grief Matters: The Australian Journal of Grief and Bereavement
http://www.grief.org.au/grief_matters.html

Illness, Crisis & Loss
http://baywood.com/journals/

Journal of Loss and Trauma: International Perspectives on Stress and Coping
http://www.tandf.co.uk/journals/titles/15325024.asp

Mortality
http://www.tandf.co.uk/journals/titles/13576275.asp

OMEGA – Journal of Death and Dying
http://baywood.com/journals/PreviewJournals.asp?Id=0030-2228

Organisations and websites

The American Academy of Experts in Traumatic Stress http:// www.aaets.org

American Psychological Association Disaster Response Network
http://www.apa.org

Association for Death Education and Counseling (ADEC) http://www.adec.org

Australian Centre for Grief and Bereavement http://www.grief.org.au

The Compassionate Friends http://www.compassionatefriends.org

The Dougy Center for Grieving Children and Families http://www.dougy.org

Genesis Bereavement Resources http://www.genesis-resources.com

Gift from Within http://www.giftfromwithin.org

International Critical Incident Stress Foundation http://www.icisf.org

The International Work Group on Death, Dying and Bereavement
http://www.iwgddb.org

Living with Loss Foundation http://www.livingwithloss.org
National Center for Post-Traumatic Stress Disorders http://www.ncptsd.org

The Solace Tree (for grieving children and adolescents)
http://www.solacetree.org

Tragedy Assistance Program for Survivors, Inc http://www.taps.org

The Workplace Trauma Center http://www.workplacetraumacenter.com

Conclusion

Crisis intervention is an approach to helping people in distress that has often been misunderstood and oversimplified. What this book has, I hope, suceeded in doing is to clear up some of those misunderstandings and present a strong case for the increased and more informed use of crisis theory in practice. What remains for me to do now is to recap briefly on the ground covered by way of conclusion.

Crisis intervention refers to the process of drawing on crisis theory concepts and principles in our work with individuals and groups at significant times of acute distress in their lives. I have argued that the term 'crisis intervention' is often misleadingly applied to a strategy of harm reduction geared towards making a crisis as painless as possible. I prefer to refer to this as 'crisis survival' and reject it as a failure to realise the positive potential of crisis intervention. 'Dealing with crises' and 'doing crisis intervention' are not necessarily the same thing.

I also argued that traditional crisis theory has failed to keep up with developments in theory, policy and practice. In particular, crisis theory, as originally formulated, is inconsistent with anti-discriminatory practice. Its focus is too narrow and individualistic (or, at most, familial) to do justice to the impact of wider cultural, structural, economic and political factors on the 'crisis matrix'. What has been propounded, therefore, is the need to update, amend and extend crisis theory so that it takes fuller account of the sociological dimension of crisis, specifically issues of discrimination on the grounds of gender, race/ethnicity, age and so on.

Similarly, a case was made for deepening traditional crisis theory by incorporating within its framework an understanding of the existential aspects of crisis – that is, issues of meaning, purpose, anguish and threatened identity. Their absence from early formulations of crisis theory can be seen as a significant weakness.

However, despite these gaps and inadequacies, it would be a mistake of major proportions to reject crisis theory in total. The line of argument here is that the immense value of crisis theory is such that it justifies the effort of 'reconstruction' to make it compatible with the strengths of current thinking.

One aspect of crisis intervention which contributes to its appeal is its emphasis on the positive. Crisis intervention, as Chapter 2 stressed, is an attempt to maximise the positive potential of crisis, to turn danger into opportunity, threat into growth. The beauty of crisis intervention is that it is not 'exclusive' – that is, it does not preclude the use of other approaches or therapeutic tools. Crisis intervention does not seek to replace other 'tools of intervention', but rather to enhance them, to provide a framework of understanding to guide their use.

A key part of effective crisis intervention is the need for rapid, yet accurate assessment. Chapter 3 discussed the principles of good assessment, the skills needed to undertake such work and the pitfalls waiting for us if we are not careful. A similar approach to the intervention phase was taken in Chapter 4, focusing once again on principles of good practice, the skills required and the pitfalls to be avoided.

Having covered the basics of theory and practice, I then moved on to present illustrations of crisis intervention in action in Chapter 5. Three case studies were used to exemplify the use of crisis intervention techniques in practice and to flag up important points about the process of integrating theory and practice. It is to be hoped that this chapter helped to bring some of the issues to life and thus bring about a better understanding of crisis intervention.

In Chapter 6 I gave an overview of some important implications of using a crisis intervention approach, such as the potential for aggression and violence and the need for work to be allocated fairly rapidly if we are not to 'miss the boat' in terms of the energy resources generated by the crisis event.

In Part Three of the book we explored issues of equality, with Chapter 7 focusing on anti-discriminatory practice in general and Chapter 8 exploring empowerment in particular. These two chapters are, in my view, an important counterbalance to the traditional narrow focus of crisis intervention. Over the years we have made significant progress towards making professional practice more emancipatory by being more aware of the significance of discrimination and oppression. However, it also has to be recognised that we still have a long way to go in this regard.

Part Four offered guidance on further learning. By its very nature this is an introductory book, but it will show how complex and multilayered crisis intervention work is. Part Four was therefore provided as a foundation for taking the learning further, using the book as a gateway to more advanced understanding and practice.

Overall, I have tried to paint a picture of crisis intervention as a helpful, if demanding, method of working with people in difficulties and distress, a means of trying to capitalise on the positive potential of crisis. As such, it can be an excellent basis for promoting empowerment.

Paradoxically, crises are both usual and unusual. They are, by definition, unusual in the sense that they represent a breakdown of homeostasis, a disruption of routine coping methods. In another sense, however, they are quite usual – especially for members of the helping professions – in that they are frequently encountered. Crisis theory teaches us to understand both the specifics of a crisis situation (the unusual), as each crisis contains unique elements, and the commonalities (the usual), as the broad trends and tendencies of crisis are readily discernible.

It is at times of crisis that the deepest pain is felt and the full intensity of human suffering can be experienced. It is a time also when human compassion can be most appreciated and most effective. Furthermore, as I have emphasised, crisis is the point at which the potential for growth and enhancement is at its greatest. The art of the crisis worker revolves around helping to guide people from the pain, grief and hurt, through compassion and onwards to growth, opportunity and empowerment.

References

Adams, R. (2008) *Empowerment, Participation and Social Work*, 4th edn, Basingstoke, Palgrave Macmillan.

Aguilera, D.C. (1998) *Crisis Intervention: Theory and Methodology*, St Louis, Mosby.

Appignanesi, R. and Zarate, O. (2006) *Introducing Existentialism*, Cambridge, Icon Books.

Aries, P. (1991) *The Hour of Our Death*, Oxford and New York, Oxford University Press.

Attig, T. (1996) *How We Grieve: Relearning the World*, Oxford and New York, NY, Oxford University Press.

Attig, T. (2000) *The Heart of Grief: Death and the Search for Lasting Love*, Oxford University Press, Oxford and New York, NY.

Attig, T. (2001) 'Relearning the World: Making and Finding Meanings', in Neimeyer (2001).

Baker, J., Lynch, K., Cantillon, S. and Walsh, J. (2004) *Equality: From Theory to Action*, Basingstoke, Palgrave Macmillan.

Barnes, H. E. (1974) *Sartre*, London, Fontana.

Barnes, M. and Bowl, R. (2001) *Taking Over the Asylum: Empowerment and Mental Health*, Basingstoke, Palgrave Macmillan.

Bateman, N. (2000) *Advocacy Skills for Health and Social Care Professionals*, London, Jessica Kingsley Publishers.

Baxter, C. (ed.) (2001) *Managing Diversity and Inequality in Health Care*, Oxford, Bailliere Tindall.

Berzoff, J. and Silverman, P.R. (eds) (2004) *Living with Dying: A Handbook for End-of-Life Healthcare Practitioners*, New York, NY, Columbia University Press.

Booker, O. (2004) *Averting Aggression*, 2nd edn, Lyme Regis, Russell House Publishing.

Bracken, P. (2002) *Trauma: Culture, Meaning and Philosophy*, London, Whurr.

Brewin, C.R. (2003) *Posttraumatic Stress Disorder: Malady or Myth*, New Haven, CT, Yale University Press.

Brown, G. W. and Harris, T. (1978) *The Social Origins of Depression: A Study of Psychiatric Disorder in Women*, London, Tavistock.

Butcher, J. N. and Maudal, G. R. (1976) 'Crisis Intervention', in Weiner, (1976).

Calhoun, L.G. and Tedeschi, R.G. (1999) *Facilitating Posttraumatic Growth: A Clinician's Guide*, Mahwah, NJ, Lawrence Erlbaum Associates.

Caplan, G. (1961) *An Approach to Community Mental Health*, New York, NY, Grune and Stratton.

Caplan, G. (1964) *Principles of Preventive Psychiatry*, London, Tavistock.

Castiglione, D., van Deth, J.W. and Wolleb, G. (eds) (2008) *The Handbook of Social Capital*, Oxford, Oxford University Press.

Clark, J. and Linsley, P. (2006) *Violence and Aggression in the Workplace: A Practical Guide for All Healthcare Staff*, London, Radcliffe Publishing.

Cloke, K. and Goldsmith, J. (2005) *Resolving Conflicts at Work: Eight Strategies for Everyone on the Job*, New York, NY, Jossey Bass.

Connell, R.W. (2002) *Gender*, Cambridge, Polity.

Corr, C.A., McNabe, C. and Corr, D. (2008) *Death and Dying, Life and Living*, 8th edn, Belmont, CA, Thomson Wadsworth.

Cranwell-Ward, J. and Abbey, A. (2005) *Organizational Stress*, Basingstoke, Palgrave Macmillan.

Cranny-Francis, A., Waring, W., Stavropoulos, P. and Kirkby, J. (2003) *Gender Studies: Terms and Debates*, Basingstoke, Palgrave Macmillan.

DeSpelder, L.A. and Strickland, A. (2007) *The Last Dance: Encountering Death and Dying*, 7th edn, New York, NY, McGraw-Hill.

Doel, M. (2005) *Using Groupwork*, London, Routledge.

Durkheim, E. (1952) *Suicide: A Study in Sociology*, London, Routledge and Kegan Paul.

Echterling, L.G., Presbury, J.H. and Edson, McKee, J. (2004) *Crisis Intervention: Promoting Resilience and Resolution in Troubled Times*, New York, NY, Prentice Hall.

Egan, G. (2006) *The Skilled Helper*,7th edn, Pacific Grove, CA, Brooks/Cole.

Erikson, E. (1977) *Childhood and Society*, London, Fontana.

Ettorre, B. (1989) 'Women, Substance Abuse and Self-Help', in MacGregor (1989).

Everly, G. S. Jr, Lating, J. M. and Mitchell, J. T. (2008) 'Innovations in Group Crisis Intervention', in Roberts (2008).

Everstine, D. S. and Everstine, L. (2006) *Strategic Interventions for People in Crisis, Trauma and Disaster*, London, Routledge.

Ewing, C. P. (1978) *Crisis Intervention as Psychotherapy,* Oxford, Oxford University Press.

Finch, J. and Groves, D. (eds) (1983) *A Labour of Love*, London, Routledge.

Greene, G. J., Lee, M-Y., Trask, R. and Rheinscheld, J. (2008) 'How to Work with Clients' Strengths in Crisis Intervention', in Roberts (2008).

Harvey, J.H. (2002) *Perspectives on Loss and Trauma: Assaults on the Self*, Thousand Oaks, CA, Sage.

Herman, J.L. (2001) *Trauma and Recovery: From Domestic Abuse to Political Terror*, London, Pandora.

Howarth, G. (2007) *Death and Dying: A Sociological Introduction*, Cambridge, Polity.

James, R.K. (2000) *Crisis Intervention Strategies*, Belmont, CA, Wadsworth.

Kanel, K. (2006) *A Guide to Crisis Intervention*, Pacific Grove, CA, Brooks/Cole.

Kellehear, A. (2005) *Compassionate Cities: Public Health and End-of-Life Care*, London and New York, NY, Routledge.

Kessler, R.C. (2003) 'Epidemiology of Women and Depression', *Journal of Affective Disorders*, 74(1).

Klass, D. Silverman, P.R. and Nickman, S. (eds) (1996) *Continuing Bonds: New Understandings of Grief*, Washington DC, Taylor and Francis.

Langsley, D. and Kaplan, D. (1968) *The Treatment of Families in Crisis*, New York, NY, Grune and Stratton.

Lattanzi-Licht, M. and Doka, K.J. (eds), (2003), *Living With Grief: Coping With Public Tragedy*, New York, NY, Brunner Routledge

Leach, J. (1994) *Survival Psychology*, London, Macmillan.

Leonard, P. (1997) *Postmodern Welfare: Reconstructing an Emancipatory Project*, London, Sage.

Lindemann, E. (1944) 'Symptamotology and Management of Acute Grief', *American Journal of Psychiatry*, No 101.

Lindemann, E. (1965) 'Theoretical Explorations', in Parad (1965).

Linhorst, D.M. (2006) *Empowering People with Mental Illness: A Practical Guide*, Oxford, Oxford University Press.

Lukes, S. (2005) *Power: A Radical View*, 2nd edn, Basingstoke, Palgrave Macmillan.

Marris, P. (1986) *Loss and Change*, London, Routledge and Kegan Paul.

Marsh, P. and Doel, M. (2005) *The Task Centred Book*, London, Routledge.

May, R., Angel, A. and Ellenberger, H. F. (1958) *Existence: A New Dimension in Psychiatry and Psychology*, New York, NY, Basic Books.

McLeod, J. (2009) *An Introduction to Counselling*, 4th edn, Maidenhead, Open University Press.

Mehrabian, A. (2007) *Nonverbal Communication*, London, Aldine.

Miller, W.R. and Rollnick, S. (2002) *Motivational Interviewing: Preparing People for Change*, 2nd edn, New York, NY, Guilford Press.

Mills, C. W. (1970) *The Sociological Imagination*, Harmondsworth, Penguin.

Mitchell, R., Dorling, D. and Shaw, M. (2000) *Reducing Health Inequalities in Britain*, York, Joseph Rowntree Foundation.

Morrice, J. K. W. (1976) *Crisis Intervention: Studies in Community Care*, London, Pergamon.

Moss, B. (2005) *Religion and Spirituality*, Lyme Regis, Russell House Publishing.

Moss, B. (2007) Values, Lyme Regis, Russell House Publishing.

Mullaly, B. (2002) *Challenging Oppression: A Critical Social Work Approach*, Oxford, Oxford University Press.

Myers, S. (2007) *Solution-focused Approaches*, Lyme Regis, Russell House Publishing.

Neimeyer, R.A. (2000) *Lessons of Loss: A Guide to Coping*, Memphis, TN, Center for the Study of Loss and Transition.

Neimeyer, R.A. (ed.) (2001) *Meaning Reconstruction and the Experience of Loss*, Washington DC, American Psychological Association.

Newhill, C.E. (2004) *Client Violence in Social Work Practice: Prevention, Intervention, and Research*, New York, NY, Guilford Press.

Nolan, M., Hanson, E. Grant, G. and Keady, J. (2007) *User Participation in Health and Social Care Research*, Maidenhead, Open University Press.

O'Hagan, K. (1986) *Crisis Intervention in Social Services*, Basingstoke, Macmilan.

Palmer, S. and Cooper, C. L. (2007) *How to Deal with Stress*, London, Kogan Page,

Parad, H. J. (ed.) (1965) *Crisis Intervention*, New York, NY, Family Service Association of America.

Raphael, B. (1990) *When Disaster Strikes: A Handbook for the Caring Professions*, London, Unwin Hyman.

Roberts, A. R. (ed.) (2005) *Crisis Intervention Handbook: Assessment, Treatment and Research*, 3rd edn, Oxford, Oxford University Press.

Rose, R. and Philpot, T. (2008) *The Child's Own Story: Life Story Work with Traumatized Children*, London, Jessica Kingsley.

Rosen, G. M, (ed), (2004), *Posttraumatic Stress Disorder: Issues and Controversies*, Chichester, John Wiley and Sons Ltd.

Ryan, A. (1988) *Blaming the Victim: Ideology Serves the Establishment*, 2nd edn, London, Pantheon.

Rymaszewska, J. And Philpot, T. (2005) *Reaching the Vulnerable Child: Therapy with Traumatized Children,* London, Jessica Kingsley.

Saleebey, D. (2008) *The Strengths Perspective in Social Work Practice*, 5th edn, London, Pearson Education.

Sartre, J-P. (1958) *Being and Nothingness*, London, Methuen.

Sartre, J-P. (1976) *Critique of Dialectical Reason: Volume 1*, London, Verso.

Scott, M.J. and Palmer, S. (eds) (2000) *Trauma and Post-traumatic Stress Disorder*, Thousand Oaks, CA and London, Sage.

Seligson, B. (1987) *Crisis Intervention: The Concept and Approach of Dr. Nira Kfir*, Wendover, Adlerian Publications.

Sheldon, B. (1982) *Behaviour Modification*, London, Tavistock.

Solomon, M.F. and Siegel, D.J. (2003) *Healing Trauma: Attachment, Mind, Body and Brain*, New York, NY, W.W. Norton.

Solomos, J. (2003) Race and Racism in Britain, 3rd edn, Basingstoke, Palgrave Macmillan.

Stepney, P. and Ford, D. (eds) (2000) *Social Work Models, Methods and Theories: A Framework for Practice*, Lyme Regis, Russell House Publishing.

Sunderland, J. (2004) *Gendered Discourses*, Basingstoke, Palgrave Macmillan.

Sutherland, V. J. and Cooper, C. L. (2000) *Strategic Stress Management: An Organizational Response*, London, Macmillan.

Swain, J., French. S., Barnes, C. and Thomas, C. (eds) (2004) *Disabling Barriers – Enabling Environments*, 2nd edn, London, Sage.

Thompson, N. (1992) *Existentialism and Social Work*, Aldershot, Ashgate.

Thompson, N. (1999) *Stress Matters*, Birmingham, Pepar Publications.

Thompson, N. (2000a) *Theory and Practice in the Human Services*, 2nd edn, Buckingham, Open University Press.

Thompson, N. (2000b) *Tackling Bullying and Harassment in the Workplace*, Birmingham, Pepar Publications.

Thompson, N. (ed.) (2002) *Loss and Grief: A Guide for Human Services* Practitioners, Basingstoke, Palgrave Macmillan.

Thompson, N. (2006a) *Anti-discriminatory Practice*, 4th edn, Basingstoke, Palgrave Macmillan.

Thompson, N. (2006b) People Problems, Basingstoke, Palgrave Macmillan.

Thompson, N. (2007) *Power and Empowerment*, Lyme Regis, Russell House Publishing.

Thompson, N. (2009a) *Understanding Social Work*, 3rd edn, Basingstoke, Palgrave Macmillan.

Thompson, N. (2009b) *People Skills*, 3rd edn, Basingstoke, Palgrave Macmillan.

Thompson, N. (2009c) *Practising Social Work: Meeting the Professional Challenge*, Basingstoke, Palgrave Macmillan.

Thompson, N. (2009d) *Loss, Grief and Trauma in the Workplace*, Amityville, NY, Baywood.

Thompson, N. (2010) *Theorizing Social Work Practice*, Basingstoke, Palgrave Macmillan.

Thompson, N. (2011a) *Promoting Equality: Working with Difference and Diversity*, 3rd edn, Basingstoke, Palgrave Macmillan.

Thompson, N. (2011b) *Effective Communication*, 2nd edn, Basingstoke, Palgrave Macmillan.

Thompson, N. and Bates, J. (eds) (2009) *Promoting Workplace Well-being*, Basingstoke, Palgrave Macmillan

Thompson, N., Murphy, M. and Stradling, S. (1996) *Meeting the Stress Challenge*, Lyme Regis, Russell House Publishing.

Thompson, N. and Thompson, S. (2008b) *The Social Work Companion*, Basingstoke, Palgrave Macmillan.

Thompson, S. (2005) *Age Discrimination,* Lyme Regis, Russell House Publishing.

Thompson, S. and Thompson, N. (2008a) *The Critically Reflective Practitioner,* Basingstoke, Palgrave Macmillan.

Tomlinson, P. (2004) *Therapeutic Approaches in Work with Traumatized Children and Young People: Theory and Practice,* London, Jessica Kingsley.

Tomlinson, P. and Philpot, T. (2008) *A Child's Journey to Recovery: Assessment and Planning with Traumatized Children,* London, Jessica Kingsley.

Van Deurzen, E. and Arnold-Baker, C. (2005) *Existential Perspectives on Human Issues: A Handbook for Therapeutic Practice,* Basingstoke, Palgrave Macmillan.

Warren, M.P. (2006) *From Trauma to Transformation,* Carmarthen, Crown House.

Westbrook, D., Kennerley, H. and Kirk, J. (2007) *An Introduction to Cognitive Behaviour Therapy: Skills and Applications,* 2nd edn, London, Sage.

Westwood, S. (2002) *Power and the Social,* London, Routledge.

Index

TiP Theory into Practice

Other books in this series include:

Religion and Spirituality
By Bernard Moss   978-1-903855-57-7 2005

Values
By Bernard Moss   978-1-903855-89-8 2007

Age Discrimination
By Sue Thompson   978-1-903855-58-4 2005

Safeguarding Adults
By Jackie Martin   978-1-903855-98-0 2005

Power and Empowerment
By Neil Thompson   978-1-903855-99-7 2007

Solution-focused Approaches
By Steve Myers   978-1-903855-18-8 2008

Full details can be found at www.russellhouse.co.uk and we are always
pleased to send out information to you by post.
Our contact details are at the front of this book.

Learning for Practice

Is a series of learning and development resources to be published by Russell House Publishing under the guidance of series editor Neil Thompson. Each manual will offer invaluable support and guidance for training and development staff in organisations; lecturers and tutors in colleges and universities; and managers keen to play an active role in promoting learning within their team or staff group.

Meaning and values
By Bernard Moss and Neil Thompson   978-1-905541-31-7 2008

Working with Adults
By Jackie Martin and Sue Thompson   978-1-905541-39-3 2008

Tackling bullying and harassment in the workplace
By Neil Thompson   978-1-905541-44-7 2009

Promoting equality, valuing diversity
By Neil Thompson   978-1-905541-49-2 2009

Responding to Loss
By Bernard Moss   978-1-905541-58-4 2010

Developing Leadership
By Peter Gilbert and Neil Thompson   978-1-905541-61-4 2010

Supervision Skills
By Neil Thompson and Peter Gilbert   978-1-905541-62-1 2011

Further manuals are planned. Details will be available at www.russellhouse.co.uk